Never Let Me Go

Never Let Me Go

A Portrait of Sexual Predation

Chuck Rosenthal

Red Hen Press ❦ Los Angeles

Never Let Me Go

Author's Note
The following story is true. To protect the victims, the names
of characters have been changed, some incidental facts altered,
and the names of locations and institutions made up or changed.

Book design by Mark E. Cull and Michael Vukadinovich
Cover design by Mark E. Cull
Author photo by Gary Goldstein
Cover photo "Boy on Bench" by Coral von Zumwalt

ISBN 1-888996-93-5
Library of Congress Catalog Card Number 2004096199

The City of Los Angeles Cultural Affairs Department,
California Arts Council and
the Los Angeles County Arts Commission
partially support Red Hen Press.

Printed in Canada

First Edition

Red Hen Press
www.redhen.org

Do not choose a coward's explanation
  That hides behind the cause and the effect

          Leonard Cohen
          "Alexandra Leaving"

For my mother and father
For Gail and Marlena

Chapter One

Dan Callahan was not the giant of my dreams. He stood five-eight, was losing his short, dark hair; he had a pot belly. He wore slacks, dress shoes, and a pale, green V-neck wool sweater over a white nylon button-down shirt and clip-on tie. His head was small and he wore glasses. His little hands, which he threw in front of him as he spoke, had thin, crooked fingers which bent backward, opposite from the natural bend of his knuckles. He did not carry a whistle, but his voice boomed as he paced back and forth in front of the bleachers.

"My last basketball team here at Holy Name was undefeated, gentlemen," said Callahan. "*Undefeated.* The last football team I coached here went unbeaten, untied, and un-scored-upon." He strode. He met everyone's eyes. "I did not return here for mediocrity. I will tolerate neither failure nor defeat. I will not tolerate the losing attitude of the last half-decade." He stopped and turned toward us, raising his hand in front of his chest as if parting the sea of bodies in front of him into mediocrity and excellence. "We will win games, gentlemen. We will win championships. You will rise to my level of excellence," he said, "or you will be gone."

He'd returned to resurrect a parochial grade school athletic program in Stuben, Ohio where sports meant everything, in a state which played a tournament to crown a grade school state basketball champion. Since he'd left five years ago our football program had sunk below mediocrity and we hadn't won a city basketball championship since Callahan walked out the door. Our cross-town rival, St. Peter's, had taken the title each year since, winning the state championship the last two.

Inside that whirlpool of chagrin I'd seen my dreams of stardom fade. At the city track championships I'd found out I wasn't the fastest kid in the city. In the sixth grade I failed to make both the football and basketball teams. Now, in seventh grade, I didn't play for our miserable football team until the last game of the season and on the opening play I broke my hand. Though only a boy, I saw my life disintegrating. But now Callahan was back. Back to turn everything around. I showed up for basketball try-outs with a cast on my right arm.

Callahan called out ten names, mine included, and sent us into a scrimmage. When I got up he stopped me.

"You can't play like that," he said.

"What choice do I have?"

"That's a good answer. Now sit down and watch the scrimmage with me."

I sat on the bottom, wooden bleacher as Callahan paced back and forth watching the scrimmage, one arm across his stomach, the other hand massaging his cheeks. Occasionally he sat down next to me, but soon he'd be up again, pacing the sidelines. "Nice shot, Mr. Richie," he said. He always called everyone Mister. "Now play some defense." Then he substituted, assigned positions and matched players up in man-to-man. He turned and looked at me. "This is not basketball," he said. "It's a travesty."

In a short while he stopped play again and began sending in the sixth and seventh graders. After that he sat down. He groaned as he watched them play. "Jesus," he said. "What a bunch of scuboogees."

He stood. "Mr. Luciani, what game are we playing?"

"Basketball?" said Luciani.

"Just checking," said Callahan.

He sat down again. On the back of his neck, his skin flaked raw against his white collar. "Are you better than them, Mr. Rosenthal?" he said to me.

Knowing he thought they were lousy, I hesitated. "Better than some," I finally said.

"Pardon?" said Callahan. Then he turned away. "Never mind," he said. He spoke to me as he watched the scrimmage. "You're in luck, Mr. Rosenthal," said Callahan. "As bad as the eighth graders are, the seventh graders are worse." He turned and raised a crooked index finger toward me emphatically. "But the barbarians are at the gate, Mr. Rosenthal. They are at the gate. Will you give your body for Rome?" He turned away, again speaking to the court. "Think like Achilles, Mr. Rosenthal," said Callahan. "Better greatness and death than mediocrity."

Each day I ran to peddle my paper routes after school, then rushed to basketball practice, dressing hurriedly in the crowded, basement locker room, then hustling up to the hot little gym; the oily wooden floor, square white backboards behind the orange rims; winter light filtered through the tall windows.

Callahan believed you didn't learn basketball in pieces; you couldn't perfect the pieces and then try to put them back together into a whole, so there were few regimens besides shooting and fast break drills. We ran laps, sprinted, and scrimmaged half court, then full. I ran with desperation. Even in my cast I won the sprints and outran everyone when we ran laps. Callahan berated the able-bodied for not beating me. "My fastest player has one arm!" he yelled.

When things went well, Callahan roared his approval. When they went poorly, he exploded with rage. Often enough he strode onto the court, red-faced, his crooked hands launched in front of him, to berate what he called bonehead plays. He seldom cursed. And if anything, the fact that he came to the gym in a shirt and tie, wearing either a suit jacket or a sweater, made his rage all the more intimidating.

Callahan was a college history teacher and came to our practices after a day in the classroom. He was no dowdy, tweed and elbow-patch professor, but regarded himself as dapper. He drew allusions to great men, great battles, great victories and noble failures. He was not beyond physically throwing players off the floor or out of the gym, though when things went really badly, he often collapsed in laughter. His laughter was ridicule and worse than his rage.

The day my cast came off Callahan took one look at my withered hand and sent me out of the gym. "Come back when you can play," he said, suddenly even denying me laps and wind sprints. I soaked and worked my hand feverishly for two days before coming back, making sure I was dressed and ready before he arrived. He regarded the hand skeptically and put me on the floor. In that week, on the verge of our season opener, he barely commented on my play and, of course, I was afraid to speak to him. Still, I felt confident. I was a good shot. I felt good. I knew I could shoot.

On the day before handing out uniforms, Callahan pulled me aside.

"Mr. Rosenthal," said Dan Callahan, "you're not good enough to get a uniform. In a normal year I'd cut you."

He noticed my tears and waved a crooked hand at me, then turned away. "Grow up," he said. He took a step farther away before he turned to me again. "There's only one decent seventh grader, Kenny Bruce. The rest of you stink. But I have to start rebuilding for next year. The sixth grade shows promise, so you can work out with them on a developmental team. Practice is right after school before varsity practice."

"I can't play right after school," I whispered.

"What do you mean?"

"I have two paper routes."

"Quit them," Callahan said.

"My father won't let me."

"Stand up to your father," said Dan Callahan.

I hesitated, then said the thing that my parents never permitted me to say. "We're poor," I said.

"Poor?" laughed Callahan. "You don't make any money peddling papers. How poor can you be that you have to work a paper route?"

I didn't have an answer for that. "I can come as soon as I'm done peddling papers."

"What will you do on game days?"

"You're not giving me a uniform," I said.

Callahan's cheeks flushed. His hand went up to my face, his index finger rocking in front of my nose. He took a breath and lowered his hand. "You're an honest boy," he said. "Too honest, Mr. Rosenthal." He paused again. Watched me. "You have your whole life to work," said Dan Callahan. "Stand up to your father. Quit the damn paper route." He turned.

"Routes," I whispered to his back.

He spun on me vehemently. He stammered. He raised that crooked finger again, then turned and walked away.

I was often afraid of my father, which belied his gentleness and sense of duty, his desire for a peaceful home, and all of this belied his rage. His name was Sam. He'd fought in the Pacific in the Second World War where my mother said he'd learned to kill and since she couldn't get the killing out of him. His ancestry was

German and Jewish, though his family had been Protestant for at least a generation by the time my mother met him. Sam had strawberry blond hair, his skin was pale and freckled. He had a slight curvature of the spine and a consequent protrusion of the stomach, something three of his children, one of them, me, inherited. Sam's father was a short, dapper man and easy-going. Sam, like his mother, was huge with a quick temper. At six feet, he'd weighed 220 pounds in the Marines. Huge then, he was bigger now.

He fell in love with Helen, my mother, in high school, at the end of the Depression, and they married before he left for the war. Their passion and the passion of the times obscured the fact that my mother was a hard-line Polish Catholic, though her own ancestors converted from Judaism during one of the many European pogroms. I suppose that made their Catholicism all the more staunch.

When my father came back from the war my older brother, Sam Jr., was already three years old. My mother's mother and brother were living with her and Sam Jr., raising him Catholic. Sam threw his mother-in-law and brother-in-law out of the house. He renamed my older brother, Gil. The families fought bitterly ever since. My parents spawned six kids in the maelstrom. I was the third.

Sam had just come off unemployment and taken a job selling toilet supplies. Gil worked in a butcher shop after school and on weekends. My older sister, Aubrey, worked behind a donut counter. I worked two paper routes, the second under a pseudonym, and my little sister, Sylvie, worked a third route that I fronted under yet another name. My youngest brothers, Joe and Andy, had just started school and now Helen was contemplating going back to work.

Upstairs in our house we had three small bedrooms and one bath, no electrical receptacles and only one light in each room, and no heat. I lived in a room with my three brothers. We had two bunk beds and no closet.

So I went first to my mother whose brother had played basketball in high school and college. Though only forty-three she was already gray. She had piercing, dark eyes. She sat me down on the couch and took my hand.

"Chuck, she said, "your father was raised in the Depression. He gave up football to set pins and work at the Forge."

I knew the story. And on weekends, between jobs, he sneaked to Miller's Field where he blasted through Stuben Academy's football team that went on to win two state titles without him.

"You have an obligation to your family," said my mother.

"It's the most important thing in the world," I said.

"It seems like it now," said Helen. "But it's not."

"I've seen every home game since first grade."

"You can still go to the games after work."

"Mom," I said. "Mom, I could make the team. I could play on the *team*. Talk to him," I said.

"To your father?" she said. "Me?"

I sat through dinner and afterward she pulled Sam aside. Then I followed her into the kitchen. She opened the gas oven and lit it to warm the air, then began washing dishes. I took up a dish towel and dried.

"You have football," she finally said to me. "It's more than he had."

I cried that night, but the next day I peddled papers and got to practice late. I stood at the gym door in my hand-me-down winter coat, my orange paper bags slung criss-cross in front of me like bandoleers.

Practice stopped. The gymnasium went silent but for the thumping dribble of a single basketball. Callahan looked toward the door. "Don't bother suiting up," he said. "Don't even bother."

Chapter Two

That November, John Kennedy was assassinated. My mother cried. "It's the end of everything," she whispered. I peddled my paper routes. And I went to every home basketball game. I couldn't put the dream away. Callahan got the school to order new red, sleeveless uniforms with gold numerals, though they retained the gold, satin jackets with *The Knights of Most Holy Name* on the back. I dreamed of wearing one of those jackets one day, but I didn't have many days left. And Callahan's turn-around didn't occur over night. Holy Name lost six league games and finished fourth.

On weekends I played seventh and eighth grade basketball intramurals at Holy Name's gym. On several occasions, Callahan himself came into the gym to watch, in case he'd missed any hidden talent, even among the scuboogees who hadn't even made the developmental team. Callahan used his eighth graders as coaches for the league, and quizzed them thoroughly about the players on their teams. One afternoon I sat within ear shot of Callahan and his best player, Feldon Richie, who was my intramural coach. I tried not to look up when Callahan asked Richie who he thought was the best seventh grader in the league. Richie nodded his chin in my direction. "Rosenthal," he said.

Callahan waved him off without even looking at me. "Forget about Rosenthal," said Dan Callahan. "We already know Rosenthal is a quitter."

In the spring Big Lou Corona, our gentle, inept football coach, took over the track team. We were barely competitive, but I ran the third leg of our 4x100 relay and we consistently placed. Later that spring I qualified for the county-wide Junior Olympics, finished fourth in the hundred yard dash and won gold in the 220.

Sam drove me to the meet at the civic stadium and afterward put his hand on my shoulder and said, "Chuck, I'm proud of you."

That night I said the rosary with my mother, kneeling in votive candlelight at our dining room table, praying to the Blessed Virgin so the world would not become Communist. I was an altar boy and that spring won first prize in the diocese for my essay on "A Day in the Life of a Priest." I was named Master of Ceremonies for Holy Name's Solemn High Mass Crew. I imagined a God who watched over me and all I did. I went to church every day, took holy communion, and loved Him.

Weekends at the YMCA, after basketball, I began swimming. I progressed out of the beginner class and by summer moved into intermediate swimming. Frank, the old swim coach, asked me if I wanted to start attending the two hour workouts that the swim team held after general swim. So I served mass and peddled papers seven days a week, and once a week, on Friday nights, collected the weekly paper bill. I had daily practice for the Solemn High Mass Crew and throughout the summer I swam Monday through Saturday, three hours a day.

Old Frank had been a lightweight boxer, now he was a Christian. He had a huge, wrinkled, almost swollen, red face and a cauliflower ear. He was one of the most gentle people I ever met. We always swam nude, but there was never a moment of shame or intimidation in Frank's pool.

By the end of the summer I progressed to advanced swimming and life saving. Though a bit of a thrasher at freestyle—Frank called it the Australian Crawl—and inept at the butterfly, I swam the backstroke decently and the breaststroke well. Some days I swam two miles. Once, during water treading drills, Frank told me to put my arms in the air and handed me a Bible. "Read," he said. I read Genesis. "Look at that," said Frank. "That kid could tread water and read the whole damn Bible." When I got out of the pool and gave him back his Bible he patted me on the shoulder. He said, "Damn strongest legs I ever saw."

I never said anything to my mother about it because my Catholic cousins and neighbors weren't permitted to join the YMCA. They believed the Y made you attend Protestant religious services. It was a mortal sin for a Catholic to attend a Protestant service. My mother was married to Sam and figured that if my Catholicism could survive him on a daily basis, it could handle the YMCA, but touching Frank's *King James Bible* was taboo.

On the last day of summer swim practices, when the two fastest swimmers on the team squared off for a hundred yard grudge match, old Frank stopped them just before the start of the race. "Wait a minute," he said. "Let Rosenthal in there." They protested, saying it was their big grudge match and they didn't want a scrub involved, besides had a dollar on it. Frank said, "Heck, let him swim, I'll give the winner five." I whipped them both. When Frank went to his locker and retrieved his wallet, he gave me the slyest little half-grin.

"How did you know I could beat them?" I said.

"Hell," said Frank, raising his stop watch, "I'm the coach."

But when fall started my commitment to Solemn High Mass Crew began to interfere with swimming practice. I approached Helen who said, "Chuck, you've been called to serve. You have to choose between God and yourself."

Yet after my Junior Olympic medals Sam had changed a little bit. Gil never succeeded at anything athletic. Sam fought with him constantly about not being good at anything, not even Boy Scouts, where the two of them put in a lot of time. All that first son stuff sat hard on Gil whom Sam never forgave for being three years old when he met him. Sam dragged me along to pick up some carryout pizza and in the car told me that story about giving up football in high school and how he used to sneak off on weekends and blast through the Academy varsity.

"I know that story," I said.

"It's not a damn story. What did your mother say about swimming?"

"Choose God," I said.

"I couldn't get married in the Church, you know," said Sam.

"I know."

"I had to sign a contract saying all you kids would be raised Catholic." He parked outside the pizza place and stared out the windshield. "I ain't going to convert. If I go to hell, at least I won't end up with my in-laws."

I'd heard that before, too, in arguments with Helen. So talking to Sam like that made me nervous. I didn't get it. I was afraid he'd be mad at me soon.

That weekend I told Frank that I'd have to quit swimming to serve as an altar boy.

"You're not Jewish?" Frank said.

"No, sir. Not really."

"You black? You have the build."

"I don't think so."

"You don't think so?" said Frank. "Can't even tell. You have a Jewish name," he said.

"I have relatives, in Europe maybe," I said.

"Hell, you're an American." Frank looked down. He looked across the quiet pool. "You want to be a swimmer?" he asked me.

"I don't know," I said.

"You could be a swimmer. If that's what you want to know."

"I want to play basketball," I said.

"Well, I'm sure you could," said Frank. "Serve God. In the end, it won't matter whether you swam or not."

At the Athletic Awards Banquet that spring, Callahan spoke in front of a packed cafeteria. He stood at the podium in front of the rows of tables filled with kids, parents, priests and nuns. He straightened his suit jacket by grabbing his lapels and raised a finger until the place was silent. "Some people think it is the end for us," he said. "The suburbs are growing, the city shrinking. So it's the end of Holy Name as an athletic power. Some people," he pointed his finger to where we seventh graders sat, "think *you* are the weakest athletic class in the history of this school. But if you accept that you will be doomed to mediocrity for the rest of your lives. Let me tell you, when defeat becomes ordinary, you become ordinary; you do not exist. You *do not even exist*."

He paused and surveyed the silent hall. "And then you are nothing. Nothing." He raised his fist in the air. "Human beings are different from the other animals because we understand failure. Because we weep over what might have been. We shall all face failure some day. We shall all weep when our inevitable failures sweep us like the tides. But when will that defeat come? At the hands of what challenge? Will it be defeat in the throes of a great and noble cause, or will you look back, middle-aged and bitter, at a life of incremental surrender?

"My friends," said Callahan, "we are in this together. We will not accept defeat. We will not succumb. We will win games and people will be shocked, *shocked* at how competitive we are. We will begin to build a dynasty which will be around when St. Pete's is long forgotten. And we won't start next fall. We'll start tomorrow morning. We'll start tonight."

Callahan told stories, of Hannibal, of King Arthur and Camelot, and the recreation of Camelot by John Kennedy. He spoke of Churchill and the Battle of Britain. "Will you lie down and accept defeat?" he said. He raised his hand and chopped at the air. "Will you make defeat the pattern of your life? Or will you rise to the occasion and make this your shining moment in time. A moment that you will be able to reach back and take hold of whenever times are tough." He pointed at us again. "Take this challenge," said Callahan, "and make it your finest hour!"

We thundered him with applause. For a bunch of working class adults and kids, it was heavy verbal rain. Afterward, I tried to avoid him. Yet as much as I tried, I ran into him on the stairs just before I left.

"Well, Mr. Rosenthal," he said. "How's the newspaper business these days?"

I stammered, looking up at him, and barely uttered a word. "Okay," I managed.

Callahan smiled broadly. He proceeded past me, then stopped below me on the gray stairs. He turned, looking up. The pale ceiling light reflected off his glasses and seemed to shine there. "Well, good luck, Mr. Rosenthal. Do you play football?"

"Yes, sir."

"Yes! That's what I like to hear. Not 'Yeah,' 'Yes!' A gentleman always says, 'Yes.' What position?"

"Halfback," I said.

"Halfback. I'm impressed. But that's right, you're pretty quick. Well, let's hope those coaches of yours can turn you around next year."

"I hope so."

"They'd better, Mr. Rosenthal," said Callahan. "They'd better. Or they'll be out of a job."

That was for football, five months away. Kenny Bruce and the members of the developmental basketball squad began practice the next day.

Chapter Three

⎯⎯ ⚬❦⚬ ⎯⎯

That fall I began the year for which I'd lived my life. Every day after school I finished my paper routes and ran to football practice. I was starting at left halfback. The night before our first game against St. Leo's, a new school from the eastern suburbs of Stuben, a team that had never won a football game, I almost slept in my uniform; dark red jersey, pants, and helmet with gold numerals and gold trim. Sunday morning, after peddling papers and attending mass, I dressed and ran to Miller's Field, excited and nauseous. As we did our calisthenics under the east goal post, I gazed to the other end of the field where the ragged little St. Leo's team lined up in their khaki practice pants, sneakers, and pale yellow helmets and jerseys with simple, blue numbers.

Huffy Roberts, our dumbbell fullback who'd flunked two grades, thumped my helmet with a finger. "If we don't crush these guys," he said, "we're in fucking trouble."

We were in trouble. Raymond Luciani, our quarterback, fumbled away our opening drive on St. Leo's one yard line. They ran it back for a touchdown and we lost 13–0. The next game we were beaten 27–0 by St. Mark's. In our third game we were slaughtered in the mud by St. Dominic's, 56–0. On one extra point, when St. Dominic's was twice penalized fifteen yards, they converted a single point by running it in from thirty-two yards out. We argued, whacked and bonged each other in the huddle. We were the Eleven Stooges. We stunk.

Our next game was against Our Lady of Hope, a team which had beaten St. Dominic's. In the first half they scored three touchdowns on us without throwing a pass. Down 19–0 at halftime, we sat in a sad circle on the side of the field when Callahan approached. He stood over us, his arms folded over his chest. "Gentlemen," he

said to us, "you are a disgrace." The he pulled Lou and his assistants aside. We could see him raising that crooked finger in the
air, pointing to us and then across the field.

When Big Lou returned he told us he was making some
changes. On defense he stacked seven men on the line, backed by
one middle linebacker and one safety behind him in case they
passed. He put Huffy on one end and me on the other to stop any
end-arounds. On offense he had Raymond Luciani stand behind
the guard and the ball snapped straight to Huffy who could take it
himself or give it to me around the end.

It worked. We stopped them cold. Then Huffy ran the ball down
the field and eventually ran it in. We'd never faced an extra point
before. We got penalized for delay of game and then Huffy was
tackled short of the goal line, but we'd scored our first touchdown
ever and it was 19–6.

We stuffed them again. Again Huffy ran it down the field. The
third quarter ended. In the fourth, I ran it once, around the end,
for the longest gain of my life, then Huffy ran it in and it was 19–
12. They stopped him on the extra point, but suddenly the parents
and kids who'd gathered on our sideline began cheering, "Beat
Hope! Beat Hope!" And across the field, a bewildered silence.
When we stopped them again with less than a minute left, they
punted the ball to our thirty and the impossible lay in our hands.

Huffy took the first snap, but every kid on Hope's defense was
waiting for him. They stopped him at the line of scrimmage. When
we ran to our huddle the ref yelled in, "Twenty-five seconds. No
time-outs."

"What are we going to do?" cried Raymond Luciani, our vesti-
gial quarterback.

I looked at Huffy. "They're looking for you," I said to him.

And he said, "I know that, asshole. Go out for a pass."

In a game which had raced along like lightning, suddenly the
seconds stretched out as if you could count to ten between them.
The sidelines fell silent. Lined up in their green and gold, the best
team in the city stared across the line of scrimmage at the worst
team. They seemed as stunned as us. We broke our huddle and
moved up to the line. As the referee counted down, "five, four,
three," Huffy barked out, "Hup, hup," and took the snap.

He ran around in the backfield with every player on Our Lady of Hope chasing him. When he lofted the ball to me, I was all alone. I caught it and took off for the end zone. As I crossed the goal line and held the ball in the air, our whole team ran down the field and we all hugged there, jumping on each other, patting each other, screaming our fool heads off. And down 19–18. There was no time left and we were penalized again for delay of game. Who cared? Back in the huddle Huffy turned to me and said, "I know, you fucking asshole. Come around behind me." He took the snap, stepped toward the middle of the line, then turned and handed me the ball as I streaked around end. When I crossed the goal line, parents and kids mobbed us. We frolicked and screamed on the sideline as Big Lou tried to quiet us down. And then Callahan was there, an arm over his stomach, his other elbow propped there to hold his hand on his chin. Finally we fell silent.

"Congratulations on your comeback, gentlemen," he said. "But you didn't win. You tied." He pointed. "Look across the field."

There, the players from Our Lady of Hope circled together, heads down.

"Look at them," he said. "It's as if they lost. That's the difference between them and you. That's how far we've fallen."

But I had my first touchdown. Even if Huffy came up to me and screamed, "You only scored one. I scored two!" Sam put his arm over my shoulder as we walked back to our car. "That was great. You kids were great in the second half. Boy were they surprised over there." Though even in my jubilation, as I played out the game, I realized I didn't have the temperament for football. I wasn't angry and aggressive like Huffy, but instead played from a kind of fear.

After that, Our Lady of Hope fell apart. Big Lou added a play where Huffy faked to me around the end and gave the ball to Herbie Thomas up the middle. Huffy scored most the touchdowns, but I got a couple more. We won our next three games against weak teams and finished fifth.

We played our last game against the fifth place team from the West, St. Paul's. They stunk and we were penalized for delay of game four times for arguing in the huddle over who should score touchdowns. After Huffy got his two we moved it around and Kenny Bruce, then Raymond Luciani, and then Herbie Thomas got their first scores of the year. I scored several conversions, but as the game came to an end I felt the failure of the season. As St. Paul's mounted their last feeble possession, I blitzed and sacked their quarterback. The next play I ran in and grabbed him by the face mask and threw him to the ground.

The ref grabbed me as I stood there crying.

"You're out of the game," he said. "What the hell are you crying about?"

As the final moments ticked away, I walked off the fieled, collapsed on the sidelines and wept. I knew I would never play football again. At thirteen, all of my dreams of sports had ended with a miserable fifth-place football game against Saint Nobody. Big Lou walked up and put his arm over my shoulder.

"Not to many people cry when they win 35–0," he said.

"I just wanted to score a touchdown," I said, looking down.

"Ah, what the hell, you got your whole life," said Lou. "I'd like to play St. Dominic's now. Now we're pretty good."

"Yeah," I said.

Big Lou wouldn't get his chance. Within the week Callahan was appointed Holy Name's Athletic Director and he fired Big Lou. In his words, "We will not tolerate mediocrity, moral victories, ties, defeat, second place. We will celebrate and reward one thing and one thing only—championships."

That night after our final game, Sam and Helen asked me about the tears. I couldn't really explain it to them. "I'm going out for basketball," I told Sam. "I'm quitting the paper routes and going out for basketball."

What good people my parents were. They didn't say a word.

Chapter Four

———❦———

Whatever desperation Callahan felt for our eighth grade basketball season, he said he was preparing Holy Name for a shot at the title. In the off season he'd worked the developmental team with Kenny Bruce as playmaker, adding the already-shaving Huffy Roberts as a forward, and a new center he'd discovered in the intramural league, Stosh Wojesewski, a dark, clumsy Polish kid we called the Wooj. At 5'11" the Wooj was a good-sized thirteen year old, and over the summer and fall Callahan had taught him how to catch the ball, turn around to face the basket, and shoot a shot which he launched from behind his head and was difficult to block.

In shooting, as with most aspects of the game, Callahan was a master of working with what he had. He imposed few systems, implemented almost no drills. You learned the game by playing it. Some boys may have had better eyes than others, some may have had better form, but anyone who shot the ball a thousand times a day, using whatever strength or form they had to best get the ball to the hoop, would become a decent shot.

Callahan forbade the Wooj from playing football, and during the football season he'd taught the Wooj how to take a dribble with his right or left hand and shoot a hook shot off the backboard. I'd been in school with the Wooj for eight years and barely knew he existed. Now Callahan proclaimed that he'd be the most lethal scorer in the league and lead Holy Name to the title. If he didn't, there'd be hell to pay.

But Callahan still really only had three players, though it looked like Herbie Thomas, Huffy's seventh grade buddy, would be the fourth. That would give Callahan three kids about 5'8" and a center who was 5'11". Good average size for a grade school team. But the rest of the developmental team were sixth and seventh grade shrimps, yet to take even a whiff at puberty. And the league that year turned out to be loaded with size and talent. Almost every team had several players over six feet.

When I showed up for try-outs Callahan raised his eyebrows. "Mr. Rosenthal," he said. "Don't you have papers to peddle?"

"I quit," I said.

"Well," said Callahan, "at least you've shown you can quit things." He paused and looked around at the bleachers full of scrubs who hadn't even played for the developmental team. "We have, at the most, two spots to fill," Callahan said to the group. "And we don't need eighth graders who won't be back next year. If you're in eighth grade and there's a seventh grader almost as good as you, then expect to be cut. No crying. Be men. Expect to be cut. Okay, let's go."

We scrimmaged for hours. Simple man-to-man. First Callahan divided up the scrubs and we scrimmaged each other. Then he picked five of us to play against the sixth and seventh graders who'd already made the team. We beat them. Then he put me and Raymond Luciani on a team with the developmental players and set us against his starters. We beat them, too.

"Holy Jesus, this is depressing!" yelled Callahan. He pulled his starters aside and screamed holy hell at them, then sent them back out. As soon as they got the lead back from us, he ended the scrimmage.

At the end of the day, before he started varsity practice, he told Raymond Luciani and me that we could come back tomorrow to give him another look.

For seven years I'd watched Holy Name take the basketball floor in their gold, satin warm-up jackets and dreamed of the day I'd touch one, wear it, hold it against my skin. Now that's all I wanted. I didn't need to start. I didn't need a future. I just wanted to make the team. But everything fell on the whim of one man who tomorrow would choose whether or not I would ever play organized sports again.

Already the girls in class, who'd begun to look and dress like young women, were picking their favorites. The playful swooning and teasing which had gone on for the last couple years had become more voracious. The toughest and sexiest of them put it simply: they wanted to be around successful young men, not failures, not children. I'd heard of necking parties to which I hadn't been invited, though even Huffy Roberts and Herbie Thomas had.

I had inklings now. I began to watch Herbie Thomas's older sister, Sally, a girl with thick, blonde hair. I thought about her hair. I listened for her as she passed my pew in church; the sizzle of her nylons under her skirt as she walked. I heard she had a crush on Kenny Bruce, but a lot of girls did. I was infatuated and confused because I watched her like an animal, clueless to my lust.

The next day I showed up for try-outs on fire. By the end of the day Callahan had matched me against one of our alumni who played J.V. for St. Mike's, the local Catholic prep. I scored on him three times, twice from the outside, once on a steal. Then he scored on me and Callahan pulled me.

"What kind of slip-shod defense is that?" he said. "Sit down." And I watched until the end.

When it was over he told Luciani and me to stay. He sat us on the bleachers in the empty gym, took off his sport coat, folded it, and placed it on the top of a bleacher. He paced, pushing up his glasses, rubbing his chin. He looked at us. He looked away. I knew I'd played well enough. I knew it. Callahan looked at us again.

"I'm keeping the two of you for one reason," he finally said. "I need bodies. I need size." He turned away and put his hands on his hips, looking at the ceiling. He turned to us again. "You're lucky it's a rebuilding year. Go shower."

But when we got up to go he stopped me. "Not you, Mr. Rosenthal. You sit down."

I sat and stared up at Callahan, the most powerful man in my life. He walked up to me and put his hand under my chin, lifting my head, meeting me with his angry, brown eyes.

"Mr. Rosenthal," he said. "You stink. You can't dribble. You can't play defense. I doubt I'll ever use you. You may never get in a game. I don't even know why I'm keeping you." He paused. He kept his fingertips under my chin. "Are you Jewish, Mr. Rosenthal?"

"Hardly," I said.

He brought his hand down. "You'd be surprised what people know." He turned and walked away, then spun, finger out. "You're the last man on this team, Mr. Rosenthal. The thirteenth man on a twelve man team. You get the last uniform.

You sit at the end of the bench. Can you handle that? Can you handle that, Mr. Rosenthal?"

"Thanks, coach" I whispered. "You won't regret it."

"I hope not, Mr. Rosenthal," said Callahan. "I hope not."

Chapter Five

―❦―

We began each practice by running laps around the gym, then ran fast break drills which simulated what occurred when your team broke quickly down court with a man advantage. In all situations I played only defense, because I was a scrub, though Callahan had the manager keep score on the plywood scoreboard that stood on the stage behind one basket—the offense got a point for scoring and the defense got a point for stopping them—the losers ran laps.

Callahan's ideal offensive play was the fast break and even in our half court game we operated on the fast break concept, because he believed that grade school players weren't capable of handling the ball for long. "One pass, two passes, and the third goes out-of-bounds," said Callahan. And that's why, when possible, on defense he employed a full-court or half-court press. His philosophy was the opposite of everyone else's. He believed that his players should be selfish and look first to score, then to pass, and that the more the other team tried pass the ball, the better chance we'd win.

"Defense," said Callahan, "was 95% sweat. Offense, 95% repetition." You didn't teach fundamentals to a dozen twelve and thirteen year olds. Practice was the time to put your team together with what you had. After our two hour practices, we went home. Then Callahan invited specific individuals to come back to the gym and hone skills after supper. I was not invited.

Callahan's starters seldom practiced against his subs. Holy Name players *played* basketball, and Callahan always opened the gym to his alums. He toughened his teams against older, more athletic boys who dropped in after their high school practices. As a sub you might do a lot of sitting, but if you got to play, Callahan worked you in with the first team.

In the beginning of the season in particular, he permitted all kinds of fouls. You had to learn to play through fouls, though if someone fouled flagrantly or on purpose, he'd throw them off the floor. And Callahan never called a jump ball. All disputed possessions were fought out on the court, no holds barred, until someone came up with the basketball and the loser lay humiliated at his conqueror's feet. If, by chance, as a sub, you were filling out a team with the alums and managed to pull the basketball away from a starter, you took his place on the first team.

Callahan screamed. He cheered. He berated. He stood in front of you, his cheeks burning red, and yelled that you were an embarrassment, that you stunk, that your ineptitude and cowardice was painful and intolerable. But his praise was yet more jubilant and elevated.

As the last man I spent more time languishing than I did sweating. And as badly as I sometimes wanted to play, I feared I couldn't stand up to the pressure and deemed myself lucky to watch from the bench. I avoided jump ball situations so I wouldn't have to face playing with the first team, and when I occasionally got my shot, I was so frightened that Callahan almost immediately threw me off the floor.

The Saturday before our first game, a non-league, home opener against a small school, St. Edward's, from a lonely town in West Virginia, Callahan handed out the new, red and gold uniforms. I waited until they were all handed out and took the last one from him, the pants too tight, the jersey too large, the satin jacket so small that the sleeves barely made it over my elbows. I felt the gold satin and held the jacket up so I could read the script on the back: *The Knights of Most Holy Name.* I held it to my chest, my heart beating. It didn't matter. Nothing else mattered.

I looked up to find that I was the only one left in the locker room. Callahan stood at the door, watching me. He shook his head, smiling cryptically, and walked away.

How excited I was when we took the floor for our opening game, the bleachers packed with eight hundred cheering fans. After lay-ups I took my place on the end of the bench as our starters remained on the floor to shoot. The Wooj won the opening tip which began an endless series of fast breaks, Kenny Bruce, Huffy, and Wooj racing down the floor again and again, thumping St. Edward's by twenty-five at the half. I got in at the end of the game with twenty seconds left and never saw the ball. Afterward, in the locker room, Callahan congratulated us. "I want you to remember one thing," he said. "They stunk. Now shower up."

We leveled another small town patsy, a game in which I didn't get in at all, but then our first big test loomed: St. Augustine's of Cleveland, last year's state runner-up to St. Pete's. Callahan had coached high school football and basketball in Cleveland before he took his college teaching job in Stuben, and he knew Curly Hensen, St. Augustine's coach. He'd arranged for home and home games last year and it irked him that St. Augustine's had taken St. Pete's into overtime in the state finals last season though Holy Name had easily beaten St. Augustine's twice. Now he had a re-building project while St. Augustine's returned their six-foot center, last year's leading scorer, and their point guard. They had two forwards over five-ten.

Callahan brought in Feldon Richie, his best player from last year who was starting J.V.s for St. Mike's Prep, and had him pretend to be St. Augustine's center. Richie tore us up. Things looked so bad that the Saturday before the game Callahan held a team meeting. He told us that we didn't match up at a single position and he expected us to be plastered.

Later that evening St. Augustine's showed up and held a practice in our gym, then showered and met us down in the cafeteria where our parish threw the teams a spaghetti dinner. Suddenly, everything from the last two games was reversed. These were sophisticated, big city kids, and their easy-going friendliness only assured us that they expected to crush the daylight out of us. Though their rangy star center remained aloof, their point guard who had a brother who played for Cincinnati University, came around and talked to us and patted us on our backs. "So your coach says you stink," he said. "Is that some kind of trick?"

"No," I said, "he tells us the same thing."

He laughed. "I like you," he said. "I hope I get to kick your ass."

"You won't. I don't get in," I said.

"You never know," he answered.

Huffy Roberts scowled at me and said, "Shut up, you fuckin' asshole. The only thing you're right about is that you won't get in."

That night, at home, Sam gave me some of his classic wisdom. "They put their pants on one leg at a time," said my dad. He looked at me. "You've grown two inches. Callahan could use you."

He was right about my growth. Since the beginning of football season I'd gone from five-six, one hundred fifteen pounds, to five-eight, one-twenty-five. "I won't even play," I said.

"You never know," said Sam.

But sometimes you *do* know.

My mother hugged me. "I'm proud of you," she said.

Though I'd witnessed several big grade school basketball games, especially against St. Pete's, the intensity and pageantry of this game was something I'd never experienced, though I would again many times at Holy Name, and seldom again in my life, even in high school and college. It seemed as if we were playing for our lives. And this intensity, this passion somehow created by Callahan, filled the lives of people in the Holy Name parish for more than a generation. Whatever it had been before, now it was more. Much more. And for many, many boys, life would never again get as deep, as painful, as filled with loyalty, joy, and lust.

In the morning, the whole parish prayed for us at each, hourly Sunday mass beginning at six a.m., and after the last mass, at noon, people began to fill our little auditorium for the game. Then two bus loads of fans from Cleveland unloaded and filed into the gym. By the time we came out onto the floor for warm-ups, the bleachers were jammed and people stood behind the end lines and in the corridors, shouting and cheering as our nuns set up folding chairs on the stage to handle even more fans who crammed in.

"It's the goddamn national title," said Huffy Roberts. He was thick and red-headed, and now no longer taller than me, but I'd come to learn he could be intense and irreverent, clever, stupid and cruel all at once.

Callahan, who never wore a whistle, gathered us up and led us through the cheering crowd, hands pounding our backs as we ran down the stairs and into the locker room. There, we sat in silence, waiting for him to speak as he paced among us. He stopped. Placed his hands on his lapels.

"Today we find out what kind of men you are," said Dan Callahan. "Today. We find out." He raised his thin index finger. "What kind of men you are!" He walked to the door and turned. "They're a better team than you are. They're bigger, more experienced, more talented. They're not from some cow pasture, some farm with lights called a town. This is the real thing. You won't play anybody better." He paused again. He rubbed his chin. "These fans, your parents and classmates, don't care that you're a rebuilding team. They think you're Holy Name. They're here to witness the greatest sports tradition in this city whip the best team in Cleveland." He met everyone's eye. "Years from now, when you're out of high school, when you're men, you'll come back to this gym and there will be state championship banners hanging from the walls. Why not start now?" he said. "Why not start *now*?" He raised his fist. "Make a statement to the city. To the state. That Holy Name is back. That Holy Name is to be feared. That in the halls of St. Pete's, they'll be saying your names. *Your* names. Bruce, Roberts, Thomas, Wojesewski." He pointed at each of them. "Beat this team," he said. "Beat them."

And damn if we didn't go out there to do it. When we opened an eight point lead in the first quarter, the gymnasium shook. Curly Hensen called time out and people stomped the wooden bleachers with their feet, shouting so loudly that the principal, Sister Mary Tess, had to walk out and quiet the crowd to let St. Augustine's cheerleaders lead a cheer. Then our cheerleaders went out, though they succumbed, abandoning their version of "Two Bits—Four Bits" to simply lead the crowd in screaming, "Beat St. Augustine's!" From our huddle, I watched Sally Thomas, her breasts, her thick blonde hair, her thin legs. Though I edited the school newspaper and won every academic award the diocese offered—I even won class elections—girls now seemed to ignore me. I wondered if Sally would notice me if I got in the game.

St. Augustine's settled down. Their stars kicked in and by the second quarter they began to dominate the boards. Now St. Augustine's built an eight point lead before Kenny Bruce hit a shot, then made a steal and fed Huffy for a lay-up. Huffy hit a jumper at the buzzer and we went into the locker room down by two.

Whatever Callahan's skills as a motivator, or in teaching a system, his greatest abilities existed in his prowess as a game coach. He fearlessly called time-outs and made changes until something worked. During that halftime he let us sit in the locker room without him, and no one, not even Huffy Roberts, spoke as we quietly absorbed the fact that we'd just played the best half of our lives on our home floor and we were still down by two. They were bigger, stronger, better ball handlers and better shots. We couldn't win.

Then Callahan came in. He took off his sport coat and looked at us. "You surprised yourselves, didn't you?" he said. "You surprised yourselves." He walked between the two long benches where we sat, then turned. "Well you don't have to be better than them all year. You don't have to be better all month or all week. Not even all day. Just for a half. For twelve minutes. Twelve more minutes." He walked through us again to the other side of the room. "Now listen up."

Callahan dropped the full court press and put us in a sagging, half-court zone, leaving their off-guard, who hadn't scored at all in the first half, totally alone. "Let him go anywhere he wants," said Callahan. "Let him do what he wants. Let him shoot. Make him beat us." He told Kenny Bruce to tag their point guard as soon as he crossed half court and had Huffy and Wooj double down on their big center. That left Herbie Thomas to box out one of the big forwards and one of our little seventh graders on the other big man, but that was the best we could do.

And it worked. We shut them down. Wooj rolled left. He rolled right. He turned and hit from the key. We regained the lead. And when Curly Hensen called time out the place shook.

Curly couldn't out-coach Callahan, but he had more talent on the floor. He screamed at his off-guard to begin shooting the ball, and though the kid made only one out of four, their big forward twice rebounded over us and put the ball back in. Callahan lowered his head and covered his eyes with his hand, then looked down the bench toward the stage. It was then that I saw that Huffy Roberts had left his warm-up jacket there. It lay on the edge, about to fall under someone's feet. Callahan's eyes lit with rage as he fixed on the discarded jacket and I knew, in that moment, that he would yell out for his thirteenth man to fetch it. In front of a thousand people, including most of my family, my name would be yelled out to send me, like some team manager, to fetch Huffy's jacket. My eyes met Callahan's.

"Rosenthal!" he yelled.

If you can believe it possible, I tried to ignore him. Pretending that the crowd was too loud, I looked away.

"Rosenthal!" Callahan yelled.

I looked up.

"Come here!"

I stood, red-faced, and approached him.

"Get in there. And rebound!"

I gazed at him stupidly before he ripped off my jacket and pushed me toward the scorer's table.

"Get in!" he yelled.

I stepped toward the scorer and Callahan grabbed the back of my jersey, pulling me to him. In that split second I believed he'd already had second thoughts and I'd gained a reprieve.

"Do you know what you're supposed to do?" Callahan said.

I nodded, though I didn't know. I went to the scorer and gave my name. I didn't look up. I didn't look anywhere. But I knew my parents would see that I was going in. Wooj double-dribbled and play stopped. Callahan groaned.

When you go into a game you fall into another world. Seconds stretch out infinitely, yet minutes fly. You are filled by a roar and din which later you can never remember hearing. The buzzer sounded. The referee turned and pointed at me and I ran onto the floor.

I was afraid. I was afraid that St. Augustine's players would see right through me, right into my scuboogee heart, and just run up and take the ball away from me. On offense, if someone passed to me, I passed the ball right back. On defense I worked doggedly in the bottom of the zone, boxing out and rebounding, giving up the ball quickly to Huffy or Kenny Bruce. Slowly I began to realize that the opposing team assumed I was in there because I belonged. The next time down the floor, I took a dribble before I passed the ball right back. And once, when we were down by one, I was fouled while going for a rebound and went to the line. I stood at the foul line as the teams lined up on the lanes; the ball a huge, slippery pumpkin, and the auditorium silent. I shot. It went in. The place roared. I'd tied the game.

Callahan pulled me late in the fourth quarter when we'd fallen behind again. "We need points," he said to me, pulling me down next to him when I tried to walk back to the end of the bench. "If you'd taken a damn shot you might still be in there."

"I was afraid," I said, but he ignored me. I'd grabbed five rebounds and scored one point. We lost by two.

Afterward Callahan came into the locker room. "You have nothing to be ashamed of," he said, "aside from defeat. You played your hearts out and you lost to a better team. Get out of your uniforms and put on your practice gear. Practice starts in five minutes."

And that practice was hell. Callahan's ex-players, smelling blood after the loss, were dressed and ready for us. I spent barely a minute with the first team before Callahan screamed at me and threw me off the floor, once, twice, and again. Several times he stopped practice in disgust and put us to running laps.

"I don't care how well you play or how hard you try," yelled Callahan as we ran. "Losing will not be tolerated. Learn this. We will not lose or you'll be living in this gym."

Later in the week, when he finally gave me another shot with the starters, I played fearfully and miserably. An old nemesis of mine, a ninth grader named Johnny Mullins, took me underneath and scored on me repeatedly. Finally, when I grabbed a clean rebound, Mullins reached in and tore the ball out of my hands.

"You stink, Rosenthal!" Callahan yelled. "You're a disgrace to the game. You will never, hear me, never get back on this floor again with the first team. Never! You're through. So quit. Get out. Sit down. Get out of my sight!"

I sat on the bleachers for an hour and a half. Humiliated. Ignored. Watching. After practice, when everyone filed out of the gym, I followed Callahan, catching up to him in the hall.

He barely turned and spoke to me over his shoulder. "What do you want, Mr. Rosenthal?" said Callahan tiredly.

"I want to come back after supper," I said.

He raised an eyebrow. "You do?"

"Yes."

"You're not good enough," Callahan said. "You'll get in the way."

"I'll watch."

Callahan faced me. He unwrapped a toothpick and worked it in his teeth. "There's no future for you, Mr. Rosenthal. Do you understand that? Not on this team. Not on any team."

"You used me against St. Augustine's," I said.

"Yes," he said. "I did. I used you. But you were so afraid you never even looked at the basket."

"I won't be afraid anymore."

That made him laugh a little. "You won't, huh? Do you think you can legislate against your emotions?"

"I won't be afraid anymore," I said.

He turned away and began walking down the stairs. "Suit yourself, Mr. Rosenthal," said Dan Callahan. "Suit yourself."

Chapter Six

⸺⟨❧❧⟩⸺

You were never late for Dan Callahan and he was never on time.
Sometimes, after school, we waited as long as an hour for him to
show up for practice, though if you weren't there in the gym waiting when he burst in, starting practice before the hydraulic door
fell shut behind him, then you were expelled for the day. It's un-
clear what that meant, because no one ever missed a practice and
no one was ever late.

It was the same after supper. We waited in the dark outside
the school entryway under the cloud-filled winter sky, the school
lawn, a blanket of white snow, reflected the dim street lights.
The Wooj was there, and Huffy, and Kenny Bruce. We paced or
goofed or slapped at each other to keep warm. It was too cold
to sit still and besides, the cement steps, covered with salt to
melt the ice, would put a chill in your butt that followed you
around the rest of the night.

Callahan finally drove up in his little Ford and got out of the
car with Raymond Luciani. Callahan carried a paper cup filled
with hot coffee and Raymond ate from a bag of Red Barn french
fries. Callahan pulled out his keys and unlocked the big metal doors.

Raymond Luciani nodded at me. "What are you doing here?"
he asked. Raymond was a beautiful kid; dark, blue-eyed, with a
thick swatch of black hair that fell in a swoop over his forehead.
He had moist, pouting lips that the girls loved.

"Working out," I said. "What are you doing here?"

"You know," Raymond said to me, "Red Barn's fries are better
than McDonald's fries. I always make him take me to Red Barn."

"Callahan?" I said.

"Yeah, where you been?" said Raymond.

I'd thought Raymond Luciani was a dead-end eighth grader like me. He never played. "You working out?" I said.

He laughed. "Maybe. I'll be starting soon though. Watch."

Callahan stuck his head out the door. "Are you coming in and suiting up, Mr. Rosenthal?" he said.

That night we worked on shooting drills, right and left hand lay-ups and hooks, and a move from the corner where you faked, took two dribbles toward the backboard, and then jumped, throwing yourself out, back first, to bank in your shot on the near side of the basket. My shooting was decent enough, but I couldn't dribble left and I couldn't come close to approximating the base line move. Once, Callahan yelled at me. "Practice dribbling on your own! Quit wasting my time here!"

Briefly, we worked on protecting our dribble. Callahan put you in the center of the key with another player. You had to dribble the ball in there for a minute while the other kid tried to take the ball away. The hitch was, the person without the ball could do anything to get it: hit, slap, shove, anything but tackle you. The winner won. The loser earned a whack on the ass.

Huffy was the best. I didn't do badly. Once, Callahan even commended me for keeping the ball from the Wooj, who he then berated severely for losing to me. "He just out-toughed you," he said to Wooj. "He wanted it more." And he sent Wooj packing to the storage room at the back of the gym.

You could hear the *whack* of Callahan's hand from out on the floor. Huffy, who had none coming, turned to me. "Bare butt!" he said.

Wooj was stoic. He was a big, impenetrable, obedient kid, still oblivious to his new status as the star of the school. But Kenny Bruce trembled when he heard the smack of Callahan's hand. With me, Callahan was perfunctory. I walked in. He said, "Pull down your pants, Mr. Rosenthal." I turned my back to him and pulled down my shorts. "Jock strap, too," he said. I pulled it down. He waited. He always made you wait, because the waiting could be harder than the pain. He hit me once, and when I didn't stir, he struck hard enough the second time to make me wince.

"Have you ever been spanked, Mr. Rosenthal?" said Callahan as I pulled up my shorts.

I turned to him. "My father just punches my lights out," I said. "He doesn't waste his time." I didn't realize that I'd punned on how he'd yelled at me earlier about wasting his time, but he saw it. He raised an eyebrow. "Is that so?" he said. "Well, I never leave a mark, Mr. Rosenthal. I never leave a mark."

Kenny Bruce whimpered on his way in and wailed so woefully through the whole thing that the rest of us, Huffy, Wooj and I, fell on the floor laughing. Callahan emerged with the whimpering Kenny and surveyed us.

"Why do I spend my time with children?" he said, almost to himself. Then he dismissed everybody but Wooj, who he kept to work on his pivot moves. I stayed until the end, working on my left hand dribble. Once I looked up at the opposite end of the floor and watched the Wooj rolling left, then rolling right, Callahan prompting now, encouraging, cheering. The winter dark from the windows poured inside and seemed, almost, to dim the air. Around the bodies of Wooj and Dan Callahan the light hung like halos. Callahan tossed Wooj the ball. He looked up and met my gaze, holding me there in his attention; he, the great man, watching me; a delicate moment of fierce rapture.

Chapter Seven

In the coming weeks I never missed an after-supper practice, though everyone else but the Wooj did. Huffy Roberts, Herbie, and some of the other seventh graders occasionally showed, but they already had extra practices, right before the varsity practice, to prepare them for next year. I showed up to scrimmage against them because Callahan held to his promise of keeping me off the floor during varsity. Then I rushed home afterward to blast through dinner and homework and race back to the gym.

I played almost invisibly, with nothing to lose. Callahan ignored my mistakes, and when I played well, occasionally offered praise. Once, before our league opener against St. Mark's, playing only defense, I took the seventh grade team apart with steals and rebounds. And because Callahan always let his defensive team fast break off a rebound, I scored on the other end, too, even against Huffy. Finally, Callahan stopped practice. "Keep that up, Mr. Rosenthal," he said, "and you'll be playing with the varsity."

But I did not play with the varsity, despite my persistence during practice drills, before practice, after supper. Even after dinner, when only the Wooj and I showed, Callahan organized the workout around Wooj. Kenny Bruce came about once a week, but only when Callahan brought him in the car. Sometimes I waited alone outside the gym until Dan Callahan showed up with the Wooj, and sometimes I waited with Wooj until Callahan drove up with Raymond Luciani, munching his Red Barn french fries. Raymond was right, Callahan had begun to work him in with the first team sometimes, but after supper he just leaned on a bleacher and watched for a little while, then left without practicing.

I served as the dummy, someone to put a hand in Wooj's face when he pivoted for his shot or rolled for his hook. Callahan raged with praise when the Wooj connected, but Wooj took his punishment, too. Once, when he kept lifting his pivot foot before driving, Callahan took him into the storage room for a long time. I heard the Wooj scream, though I didn't hear any slaps. He emerged with Callahan following him, his face puffy and his eyes red. He didn't lift his pivot foot again.

When I could, I worked on my shooting, my dribbling, my moves. "I want to learn more," I said to Callahan.

And he said, "You're not ready. Besides, our season rests on those shoulders." He pointed to Wooj, who shot from the key, missed, loped after the ball and shot again, the ball flying off the back of the rim. "That body. Those legs, those hands, that limited brain." He looked at me. "You have the brain, Mr. Rosenthal. I just don't know if you have anything else."

The Wooj gathered up the ball in the corner, faked left, took a dribble to the base line and sprang out forcefully, gently banking the ball into the hoop. It was graceful. Beautiful.

"Yes!" shouted Callahan. "Yes! That was gorgeous, Mr. Wojesewski. Absolutely gorgeous. End with that. Get a shower."

Callahan seldom came down to the locker room after a practice. And in those hours waiting outside in the cold, or showering and dressing together in the basement of the school, I got to know Wooj a little. He was big and sweet. He felt and thought only one thing at a time, but felt and thought it deeply. Before this basketball season I barely knew he existed. He was in the other eighth grade class. I lived near the center of town and Wooj lived well southeast of the school. Wooj had never distinguished himself academically or athletically. He never before seemed to harbor an ambition. Now, his dark forehead brooded with the weight of Holy Name's legacy. He was averaging almost twenty points a game. He was somebody for the first time in his life. He was a star.

The winter wind whistled around the school building, coming through the old, leaky windows and moaning through the halls. We padded across the hallway wrapped in towels to shower in the boys' room which had only two shower stalls. These moments, when there weren't a dozen sweaty kids jamming and pushing at each other in that tiny bathroom, were a real pleasure for me, because we didn't have a shower at home. Wooj and I showered and dried off. Unlike me, the Wooj was already mature. He was at least two inches taller, and though his legs were slender, his biceps and neck were large and his long forearms and calves, as well as his crotch, were already thick with dark hair. This build, this lankiness, was what Callahan called a basketball build.

"I didn't hear a slap," I said to Wooj.

Wooj didn't say anything, but dried himself quietly.

"In the storage room," I said. "I didn't hear any spanking."

Wooj looked at me from under his towel as he dried his head, then he dropped his hands and put the towel around his waist. "Do you ever think, Chuck, that, well, you know, that Coach Callahan is a little weird?"

"No," I said immediately. "No. I mean, I don't know what you mean."

The Wooj just shrugged, then turned away. We dried and dressed and walked upstairs where Callahan met us in the gym. We said good night. I walked home and the Wooj went off with Callahan.

St. Mark's was our league opener and we played them in our gym. They were one of the co-favorites to challenge St. Pete's for that year's title. Like a lot of teams, St. Mark's, who'd beaten us 27–0 in football, operated around a talented point guard who'd been their quarterback and a big center who'd been their fullback.

We packed the gym again that Tuesday afternoon. I sat on the end of the bench again, though Raymond Luciani now sat next to Callahan. We couldn't stop St. Mark's, even though we were prepared, even though Callahan called early time-outs and made a number of adjustments. Wooj and Huffy played okay, but Kenny Bruce began to show his first cracks. He played horrible defense and he couldn't hit his shots. Callahan screamed at him at halftime. He moved Kenny onto a new man, but then he tore Kenny up, too. Finally, Kenny Bruce, our mainstay, our veteran, missed several open lay-ups on fast breaks, including two at the end of the game after we'd briefly taken the lead. We lost, 44–42. We stayed after, ran laps and practiced. After dinner, I went back to the gym and worked out with the Wooj while Callahan cursed Kenny Bruce's absence.

On Thursday St. Joe's came in with three kids bigger than Wooj, but they shot poorly and led us only 16–15 at the half, when Callahan put us into a zone and moved the Wooj out to the wing and let him bomb from there. We weren't getting any rebounds anyway, he said, so what the hell was the difference? Huffy did his usual, steady job. He was a son-of-a-bitch, but nothing intimidated him. The big problem was that Kenny Bruce did not score at all. Still, with fifteen seconds left, we had the ball at half court, on our own floor, down only 35–34.

Callahan called time out. He told Huffy to make the inbound pass to Wooj. "Wooj," said Callahan, "it's your game. You're the star. You be the hero."

Wooj nodded intently and the little gym, again filled with some nine hundred fans, exploded as Holy Name came out. Huffy got the ball to the Wooj who dribbled across the key. He ducked a defender and drove the base line. As the crowd began to count down from ten, Wooj, head down, dribbled to the corner.

"Shoot the ball!" yelled Callahan. "Wojesewski! Shoot the ball!"

Wooj paused, kept his dribble, and took the base line again for his patented leaping move. The crowd shouted to him, "Four! Three!" and the Wooj, reaching the basket, dribbled out to the other side as the clock ran out.

There was a moment of stunning silence as the Wooj leaped into the air, throwing the ball toward the ceiling, bouncing madly in that moment of quiet before the St. Joe's players began to hug each other. Wooj turned and looked across to Callahan, who burst red, almost tearing his hair. Even in the growing tumult from the St. Joe's fans I could hear the Wooj whisper. "I thought we were winning," said Wooj, his face dropping in singular realization. "I thought we were winning."

That night we ran again. We ran and ran. We never practiced. We just ran. The team manager changed the score on the plywood scoreboard and Callahan yelled out to the Wooj, "Mr. Wojesewski, what's the score? Who's winning?" and the Wooj moaned out the answer, at first in a kind of wail, but by the end, morbidly, in self-pitying resignation.

After a long while we noticed Callahan standing in the middle of the floor, forehead in his hand, chuckling. We all slowly stopped as he looked up at us. "Incredible!" laughed Callahan. He spread his arms. "I've never seen anything as boneheaded in my life!" He sent us home, and that night when I came back after supper, not even the Wooj showed up.

"Well, well, Mr. Rosenthal," said Callahan as he juggled his huge set of keys, laying them in one gloved palm and sifting through them with the fingers of his other hand. The steam of our breath puffed into the frigid night air. "It's down to me and you, is it? It's come to that." He looked up and gave me a faint grin, his eyebrows raising. He chuckled easily. "Of all things. Me and you."

Chapter Eight

That night after the St. Joe's game Callahan worked me with shooting drills. I shot from one corner, rebounded, then dribbled off and shot from the other corner. Surprised by my accuracy, he set me to another drill in which he rebounded the ball and threw it anywhere he wanted. I had to retrieve it and, permitted only one dribble, shoot from that spot. I played to twenty, one point for a make, one for a miss. That night I won one, then lost one. Callahan set up the rubber match. If I lost I'd be spanked, but he gave me plenty of easy shots.

Before sending me to shower he called me over.

"So," he said, "you're pretty serious after all, Mr. Rosenthal."

"Yes, sir," I said.

He strode away, then came back.

"Do you want to be a basketball player, Mr. Rosenthal?"

"Yes."

"Take your shirt off," said Callahan. "Let me show you some of what it will take."

I took off my shirt and stood in front of him.

"Give me your right arm," he said. And he took it and brought it behind my back in a hammer lock. I winced with the first shot of pain, then settled into it as he placed his index finger on my chest. "See this muscle in your chest?" he said, outlining the top of my chest with a stroke. "It's hard and bulky. A swimmer's muscle. It shouldn't go across like yours, but down, like this," he said, tracing it down. "No swimmer has ever played basketball worth a damn, Mr. Rosenthal."

He took his thumb and put it into my chest muscle. "Brace yourself," he said and pressed hard, running the thumb across my muscle until I screamed. "That's what it will take to transform your body, Mr. Rosenthal. Hours of it, day in and day out. And not just on your chest, but your neck and thighs, your buttocks. Think about it, Mr. Rosenthal. Think about it."

That night, after I showered alone, listening to the cold, moaning wind in the halls, Callahan met me outside the locker room door after I'd dressed. As we walked out, he put his hand on my shoulder. "Do you think we can beat St. Peter's?" he said.

"It's five on five," I said, mimicking my dad.

"Indeed, Mr. Rosenthal. Five on five. But their five has us beat at every position. That's why we're zoning them. When was the last time Holy Name beat St. Pete's?"

"When I was in fifth grade we beat them on their floor," I said. "And in sixth grade we beat them on ours. But we lost the play-off both years. We beat St. Paul's for the title when I was in first grade. That was your last team."

"You have a good memory," he said.

"Nobody else has beaten them in five years," I said.

"Indeed," Callahan said. He put a hand on each of my shoulders and turned me to him. "Are you ready to play?"

"Yes," I said, all too uncertainly and he laughed.

"We will fight them on the land, Mr. Rosenthal. We will fight them in the air and on the sea. We will fight them on the beaches. We will fight them in our streets." He raised a fist and smiled. "Mr. Rosenthal," he laughed, "it will be our finest hour." He turned, serious again. "Be ready," Callahan said. "Be ready."

We thought we had the finest gym in the city. It was one of only two wooden floors, though it was worn and improperly maintained by oiling it down. Unlike most schools, who used their gyms for cafeterias and school assemblies, our gym was used only for basketball, and instead of folding chairs we had bleachers. The only other school who had bleachers, as well as rectangular, not fan, backboards, was St. Pete's, though ours were wooden. St. Pete's had the only fiberglass boards in the league. They had an almost regulation-sized, green tile floor, and the league's only electric scoreboard, not the kind you see today, but an electric version of our plywood one where the painted numbers fell into place with a clunk. It had a circular time clock in its center, between the scores. They were the only school that didn't use a hand clock and shout out the time remaining.

In preparation for St. Pete's big floor, Callahan had us roll back the bleachers and practice wall to wall. Our ex-players crowded in to prepare us and pump us up.

St. Pete's was the biggest game of the year. Every year. No matter that they were 2–0 and we were 0–2. No matter what.

Still, I didn't practice with the first team until the last moments of our Monday practice before the big Tuesday game. Callahan brought me in for a few moments and let me face off with Johnny Mullins. Though the encounter was too brief for any consequence, when the scrimmage ended Mullins grabbed me and said, "If you lose to them, you fuckin' quitter, I'm going to come looking for you."

I don't know what got into me, I turned to him and said, "One, I won't play. And two, you lost to them twice." Callahan called off the after-supper workout and told everyone to rest.

Game day was electrifying. It was like a holiday in school. No one did anything but talk about the game. School released early so children fifth grade and up could get on rented busses and ferry to St. Pete's. At the game itself the bleachers were packed with fans wearing St. Pete's colors, green and white, and the place shook when they came on the floor in their old style green jerseys with sleeves and two white stripes over the shoulders, their faded, green satin jackets, worn open, flying as they took lay-ups on their end.

They had two starters from last year's State Championship team, but we knew them all. The point guard, Stumpy O'Brien, had started since sixth grade. Some people considered him the best basketball player in the city. He was the kid who, in fifth grade, beat me in the hundred yard dash. Their coach, Wally O'Hara, was a huge Irishman with a big, balding head and red face. Callahan had said little about him, but we knew he hated him.

St. Pete's scored off the opening tip. Kenny Bruce missed two lay-ups in the first quarter. The Wooj scored twice and Huffy scored, but we finished the period down 12–6. By half it was 28–11 and Callahan stormed into the locker room enraged.

"No team of mine has ever played this poorly," he roared. He reamed each of the starters individually, as well as a couple of the subs. "You will come back," he yelled. "You will make this a game or there will be hell to pay, gentlemen. Hell to pay."

During half-time warm-ups I watched from the bench as our starters shot around, then O'Hara strode onto the dark green tile court ahead of his powerful team. Their fans cheered and the players laughed and patted each other as they glanced toward our half of the floor. O'Hara gathered in his boys. He stared haughtily across the floor at Callahan.

I looked up at the famous scoreboard and our pathetic score and thought about the failure of my eighth grade class, and my failure within that failure. Then I noticed my mother in the bleachers with my younger brothers, Joe and Andy. She must have come in at halftime, catching the East Street bus after my brothers got out of school. I didn't wave, but her eyes met mine; the eyes of a mother whose son is not in the game.

The second half began. St. Pete's scored twice. Callahan tried a full-court zone press, a half-court zone press, a half-court man-to-man, but nothing worked. They were bigger, quicker, better ball-handlers, a better team playing at home. Near the end of the third quarter with the score 39–17, Callahan called time-out. O'Hara again stared at him across the floor. He tilted his head slightly, looking for a concession, because it was an unwritten law of the league that nobody pulled their starters until the losing team conceded. No surprise, then, that it produced lopsided scores, hard feelings, and vengeance among the coaches and schools.

Callahan looked down the bench. "Rosenthal," he said. "Check in."

This time I was not surprised. I remembered promising him I wouldn't be afraid and I reached inside for something I didn't know I had, something vicious and blind to anything but competition. When I checked in and got back to the huddle, I was ready. Callahan said, "We're conceding nothing." He looked at me. "Nothing!" He put us in a full-court man-to-man press. "If we go down, it will be like Valhalla. We'll go down in fire." He grabbed my arm as the teams ran out. "You run from corner to corner on offense. From one corner to the other. That's all. And when you get the ball, you shoot."

I got a break when O'Hara interpreted my insertion as a concession and put in a sub of his own, so I had an easy time on defense. And the first time down on offense, when the ball came to me in the corner, I shot it and scored my first field goal ever. I'd like to say I heard cheering, or saw my mother's face, but in fact I heard and saw nothing. The game rose over me like huge wave. We stopped them from scoring, came down again, and the ball came to me in the corner. I hit again. O'Hara screamed, "Somebody cover that little nobody!" But when their zone came out to guard me, I hit the Wooj rolling down the post and he banked in his patented hook. The buzzer went off for the end of the quarter and we were now down 39–23.

O'Hara was furious. He put his first team players back in and when one of them blew by me for a score, I was sure Callahan would pull me. But he didn't. O'Hara raged on the side line, but the tide had turned. I scored twice more, then took the base line and got fouled trying to make the push-out move, knocking down one of two from the line. Huffy hit, and the Wooj got hot, too. When the Wooj scored again with a little over a minute left, making the score 43–37, he raised his fist in the air and our fans stood screaming and applauding. O'Hara called time out.

I remember so clearly standing on that sideline drenched in sweat, the visceral press of our fans yelling down at us; it was glorious. In a moment I was no longer a quitter, nor a teacher's pet, but a member of Holy Name's basketball team. I was playing for Holy Name against St. Pete's. I was playing for Holy Name. In that moment, forgetting myself, I was so happy that I didn't even care if we won. I'd stepped into my dreams.

"They'll go into a stall," yelled Callahan above the din. "We'll have to foul."

And they did go into a stall. And we did foul. And they hit their foul shots while we rushed our shots on the offensive end. Our rally fell short. St. Peter's had beaten us again.

Despite our rally, in our locker room Callahan was merciless. "That is the worst defeat I have ever taken," he said. "You're a disgrace. Do you want to know what greatness is? *That* was greatness you played against. *That*." He paused and gazed around the room. "That was greatness. Measure yourselves. You're a disgrace to your school. A disgrace to your uniforms. Get them off. Get out of them. Now."

As we undressed, Wooj and Kenny Bruce wept. Myself, I sweated so heavily that I couldn't, as Callahan or Churchill might have said, tell the sweat from the tears.

My father worked late that night, as he often did now with his new job, selling bathroom and janitorial supplies. I didn't have homework and after supper I got dressed to go to the gym. My mother stopped me.

"Tonight?" she said.

"He didn't say no," I told her.

She pulled me toward her, a woman whose depth made the limitations of her life all the more painful to her. As a girl, she'd been successful in the limited world of female sports, briefly holding the city record for the high jump and standing broad jump. She swam well and often played football and baseball with us in the backyard. On summer afternoons she'd taught me how to scissors kick over a high jump bar and clear a hurdle in a stride, something I never mastered as well as her. A whiz at algebra and geometry, she'd studied Latin on her own and skipped two grades in school. She won a scholarship to college and turned it down to marry Sam and enter the work force during the war. To the end, she was a voracious reader, a symbol against all the stereotypes of the working class.

"Do you remember the stories about Holy Trinity winning all those championships before the Second World War?" she said.

"Yes," I said. I knew the history of grade school basketball in Stuben back to the Thirties.

"Before that it was Saint Jerome's. My school. We won all the time."

She'd gone to St. Jerome's, and her sister and brothers, too. My mother's great uncle was the Monsignor of St. Jerome's, once the cathedral of the Polish ghetto, and when Helen's mother, Frances, came over from Poland she lived and worked in the rectory until she married my Grandpa Stanley.

"I know that," I said. "But now St. Jerome's is the worst team in the league."

"St. Peter's was the worst team in the league then," she said. "They were the worst team for years."

"Now they're the best," I said.

"Yes," she said. "Now." She gave me hug. "You did well today. You love it, don't you."

"Yes," I said.

I waited outside the gym in the cold for a long time. No one came. I gazed out at the points of crystalline street light as it reflected off the murky snow, patted my arms to keep out the cold, paced, watched my powdery breath. Finally, Callahan's little car drove up to the curb. He got out with the pile of clean, folded uniforms in his arms. He looked at me and blinked.

"What the hell are you doing here?" he said.

"You didn't say there was no practice," I said to him.

He had me get the keys out of his pocket and I opened the door, then followed him down to the locker room where he put the uniforms on a bench.

"Pick out one that fits you," he said.

When I hesitated, he said, "Go ahead, pick one out. We'll get it worked out tomorrow."

I found some pants that fit me, and a big golden jacket. I found a smaller jersey which changed my number from 44 to 25. I put it on.

"Take it home," Callahan said.

I stood in front of him, appreciative, proud, and dumb.

"Did you know what I meant by Valhalla?" he said to me.

"No, sir," I said.

And he explained to me about Norse myth and Valhalla, the warrior code, about Wagner's opera and the last battle in heaven, the Twilight of the Gods. "The Twilight of the Gods," Callahan said. "Isn't that a magnificent phrase?" He raised his hand, almost kissing his fingers. "Magnificent." For all his emphasis on victory alone, so many of his stories ennobled glorious defeat. "Come on," he said. "No practice tonight. I'll drive you home."

As we walked down the hallway he put his hand on my shoulder. "Chuck Rosenthal," he said, "you played well. You didn't play scared, you played well. You met the challenge. You kept your promise. You will start against St. Dominic's."

Before our next practice the news arrived even before Callahan. St. Dominic's had upset St. Peter's. Holy Trinity had knocked off St. Mark's. Now they were both undefeated and they were our next two games away from home.

Chapter Nine

St. Dominic's gym was a band box, a little wider than ours but so short that they used an extension of the foul line in the front court for over and back. It was a dark little place with a brown tile floor and fan bank boards that folded up into the ceiling; a gym used for assemblies and cafeteria and even mass until they built their new church. That was where they'd ambushed the state champions, St. Pete's, who'd beaten us last week by seventeen.

Over the weekend Callahan barely spoke of the fact that St. Dominic's was undefeated and had knocked off St. Pete's. Neither did he speak of the 56–0 slapping they'd given us in football. To take advantage of their small court, he put us to work on a three-quarter court trap where Kenny Bruce and I doubled-teamed at their odd time-line while Wooj fronted their center. Callahan didn't care about anybody else. Huffy roved the back court to pick off passes and Herbie waited under our basket in case they broke the press. We practiced it against our alumni and failed so miserably that Callahan stopped yelling at us about it. He just watched them tear us up and stood there holding his chin.

The next day, before we left for the game, Callahan told me to shower, then he came into the bathroom and made me turn down the hot water.

"Colder," he said.

I tried, but when I wouldn't turn off the hot water he reached into the stall and turned the water on cold, full blast, and held me in. When I was soaked and shivering he pulled me out and took a scratchy towel and rubbed it vigorously over my skin. When I was good and red he said, "Come here." He held both arms behind my back by the wrists and began slapping me. He slapped me hard, my chest, stomach, thighs, butt. I yowled. He said, "Shut up." Then he rubbed me down again and stepped back. "I've noticed that you take too long to warm up," he said. "I can't have you blowing this game in the first five minutes. When you get there, warm up hard. Get a sweat." Then he pulled a Hershey bar from his pocket and handed it to me.

"Candy isn't bad for you?" I said.

He laughed. "It's the best thing in the world for quick energy. Eat it on the way there."

I nodded.

"From now on I want you to do this for yourself," he said. "Today, play the game of your life, Mr. Rosenthal. Play the game of your life."

We entered St. Dominic's gym while they were already warming up, casually tossing basketballs at the hoop and laughing. When we crossed the floor they paused for only a second before going back to shooting around. It was a moment that wasn't lost on any of us. We were Holy Name. Once we inspired fear. Now we were barely worth notice.

The whole thing grew only more dismal when we dressed and went out to warm up. We had no fans at the game. No nuns, no mothers, no alumni, no busses of classmates. Nobody had bothered to drive this far into the southwest suburbs to witness the massacre. Our cheerleaders ran through their repertoire to a silent gym, filled now with red and white streamers and pompoms, a banner that said, "St. Dominic's—1964 City Football Champions." When St. Dominic's cheerleaders took the floor everyone stood and screamed. They didn't even bother to yell "Beat Holy Name!" Callahan led us off the floor as they stomped their feet and chanted, "City Champs! City Champs!" We were 0–3. They were 4–0.

In the little storage room where we'd dressed, the pounding and cheers of St. Dominic's fans rolled through the walls. Callahan stood over us as we crowded at his feet. He let us listen. "Here that?" he said. "Are you listening to that?" He looked around. "Well, gentlemen, I am, too."

He paused again, searching each of us. "You know, gentlemen," he began, "almost two hundred years ago this country we call the United States didn't exist. Where we stand now was British, just won from the French."

Huffy Roberts started to smirk, because it was an odd time for a history lesson and only Huffy had the guts to show it, but

45

Callahan quieted him with a stare.

"During the Revolution—Mr. Roberts, you *have* heard of the American Revolution?—the American army under George Washington was defeated again and again. *Again and again.* At Boston and New York, Washington retreated and was badly beaten. The British walked into Philadelphia without a fight. Without a fight! The British controlled every major city in the colonies. The war was over. It was over. No nation had ever taken possession of every city in another country and lost a war. In fact, no one had ever done it and not had their enemy immediately surrender." He paused, both his hands raised to his shoulders. He looked around. "But Washington didn't surrender. His men were deserting. He was low on ammunition and food. The soldiers he had left were barely clothed. It was winter. We had no allies. No friends. In the spring the British would consolidate their armies and march into the countryside and clean up the remaining American combatants and that would be it."

Somehow, now, despite the pounding that came through the walls, the room fell silent. Callahan put up his index finger. "That's when Washington did the unexpected thing. On Christmas Eve, in the winter, at a time when no one fought, he gathered his troops and, ferrying his freezing men across the water on boats, crossed the ice-filled Delaware River. They could have all died there at that crossing and the Revolution would have been over. But they didn't. Washington himself led the way. He took the British fort at Princeton by surprise. He attacked a fully armed fort and took it without losing a man! He captured the ammunition, the supplies. He beat the British. He beat them when they least expected it. While they sat, overconfident, in their own fort on Christmas Eve. And with that stunning victory George Washington turned the head of every leader in the world. On that night everything changed. On that night," he paused again, "the British lost the war. And we began to win." He looked around at us. "And we did win, gentlemen," said Callahan quietly. He folded his arms in front of him. "*We* won. And you will, too." And he walked out.

As bewildered as we were inspired, we followed him out onto the floor and took our lay-ups under the quiet of our enemy's crowd, the basketball thumping in the silence until St. Dominic's hit the floor under a din of cheers. Though with me starting we were now a pretty decent sized team, with everyone at least 5'8", St. Dominic's, aside from their point guard, was still bigger than us, and in that moment I recalled the rainy Sunday that they ran onto the football field in their plain white helmets, white pants, and white jerseys, and ground us into the mud. We didn't even get them dirty. And unlike a lot of the other teams, they did no name-calling, threw no punches under the pile-ups. They thrashed us silently, too good to bother with any of that bravado, that nonsense. They were the new juggernaut. The future. The new sports dynasty. And it was evident in their carriage.

The buzzer sounded and we gathered with Callahan at the sideline, then went out. I stood outside the jump circle feeling both excitement and gloom. My first start, but in a season already marred by failure, in a game marked to seal our fate as the worst team in the history of Holy Name basketball. The referee blew his whistle and threw the ball in the air. St. Dominic's controlled the tip and went down and scored. The little gym shook with a roar. Unlike George Washington, in the opening seconds we'd already given up our first casualty.

St. Dominic's casually fell back into a zone, which was a good thing because with me on the floor, shaky Kenny Bruce was our only true ball handler. He dribbled down, threw the ball to Huffy on the wing who passed to me in the corner. I shot and scored. The gym fell silent as we went into our press. St. Dominic's star point guard's eyes widened slightly, and then he smirked. He calmly called his other guard down to take out the ball and we let him receive it without pressure until he dribbled across the time line. There, trapping him against the over-and-back line, Kenny and I doubled him and he threw the ball into Huffy's hands. Huffy hit the lay-up and we pressed again. Again we doubled-teamed at the time line and Huffy intercepted, this time passing to me in the corner. I shot and scored.

Now their point guard motioned irritably for their big center to come down and help him out, but we doubled him when he caught the ball and he dribbled it off his leg. Wooj hit from the key. Even Kenny Bruce scored on a drive. I ran the corners and hit again. And again. The ball felt like an extension of my hand, the basket an ocean.

St. Dominic's seemed too stunned to even call time-out, as if suddenly the game would right itself and come back to them as they knew it should. But we continued to scuttle them. In front of a silent, packed house, a gym full of fans who expected to witness a slaughter that would mark them as the new, odds-on city champion, they failed again and again to get the ball out of their own back court. At the end of the first quarter we led them 18–2 and I had eight points.

Between quarters St. Dominic's fans recuperated and revved up. They chanted "Beat Holy Name!" as a number of them behind our bench yelled insults about us being 0–3 and their massacre of us in football, but now that only fed us. Though they came out in the second quarter ready for the press, now managing to break it and get down the floor, our frantic double-teaming kept them rushing their shots. We rebounded and rushed back down the court, one pass, a shot, and in. In the deluge I scored three more times from the corner and when the half ended I had fourteen points and we led 40–10.

In our locker room at half-time Callahan just crossed his arms over his chest and smiled. "Well, well, gentlemen," he said. "Well, well." He stood silently for another moment. "Are you listening?" he said. "It's pretty quiet out there." Then he paused again. "Feel the pleasure, gentlemen. Don't forget this. This is the team that crushed you in football. Feel the pleasure." He nodded to me. "Nice shooting, Mr. Rosenthal," he said.

Then he got to work. In classic Callahan coaching, he did not sit back on what had succeeded in the first half, but anticipated St. Dominic's adjustments. They'd be ready for the three-quarter court trap, so we'd drop out of it. We'd press them at half court after we scored, pick them up man-to-man if we didn't. He told me that after blistering them from the corners in the first half I should expect them to come out after me. He made sure Wooj would be rolling down low and Huffy would cross into the high post to give me two possible passes inside. If those were clogged, Kenny Bruce would wait for a release pass on the wing. "All right, gentlemen," he said, "let's finish the job."

When we came out for the jump ball I lined up next to St. Dominic's point guard who offered me his hand. "Jesus," he said to me, "St. Pete's told us you guys stunk."

"We do," I said.

"This is ridiculous," he said. "It's forty to fucking ten!"

And the third quarter went exactly as Callahan predicted. Expecting the deep trap, we stunned them with our half-court press. They never figured out when we were in a zone and when we were man-to-man. Their defense came after me in the corners and left Wooj and Huffy wide open in the key. I didn't score until the end of the quarter, when they finally got tired of coming out after me only to have me dump the ball inside. I hit from the corner again. Then, just before the buzzer, I knocked down a pass and leapt out of bounds to save the ball, hitting Huffy on the fly for a lay-up at the buzzer.

At the beginning of the fourth quarter, down 58–15, mighty St. Dominic's went into a stall to hold down the score. They took the ball out and held it down on their end of the floor. They'd surrendered. Callahan sent in the subs. We'd crushed them, in their own gym, 64–23.

Kenny, Wooj, me, and even Huffy raced from Callahan's car when we got back and ran to the convent to tell the nuns. Our chubby and often dour principal, Sr. Mary Tess, came to the door of the convent and we started screaming, "We won! We won!" She called inside to the other sisters and there was a big celebration of kids and nuns screaming and hugging in the foyer. At one point Huffy slapped me on the side of the head and said, "And this asshole scored sixteen points!" There was a quiet moment and then an explosion of laughter. For an evening, we were a real team.

Callahan prepared us for Holy Trinity as if nothing big had happened and nothing big was about to occur. We learned a new zone defense to counter their size and strength. Callahan was a good teacher. He broke the game down to individual responsibilities. And he motivated you with inflationary praise when you succeeded and boisterous humiliation when you failed. He was good at what he did. He worked at it. He expected you to work as hard. He demanded excellence.

It was easy to forget that he had a real career. At St. Mary's College, he'd advanced to associate professor and then became department chair. He ran the education department, too. Eventually he got involved in local politics, where he advised the city council and one of his ex-students became mayor. He headed the Stuben Society for Historical Resoration. But in terms of basketball, he stayed with boys, to work, he said, where sports was still pure, where desire was raw and simple, where minds and bodies could be molded, and lives built.

Now that I was a starter my after-supper workouts changed. The Wooj and I played as equals, though it meant pairing off against him and at that stage he was better than me at most things. That meant more defeats and more spankings. And after the workout I'd follow Callahan to the little storage room where he put me in a hammer lock and pounded at my chest, and then, with his head on one breast, he put his thumb or knuckle deep into the muscles of the other breast and rolled them down. The pain was excruciating. Once I screamed so loud he threatened to spank me if I didn't shut up. He grabbed my testicles. "I dare you to scream now," he said. Shut up, or he'd stop for good and my fledgling basketball career would be over then and there. I'd learn, he said, like a Spartan warrior, to endure pain in silence.

That next Thursday we went to Holy Trinity with a bus load of fans. Undefeated Holy Trinity, playing at home, was bigger and stronger, but not well coached. Their guards actually laughed when we didn't come out after them. But Callahan's strategy worked again. They shot poorly against our sagging two-three zone and we beat them, 40–38, in overtime. Though I fouled out, I scored ten points and grabbed ten rebounds. In consecutive games we'd knocked two undefeated teams out of first place, and beat them on their floors.

On the following Saturday night, after Callahan completed his work on my chest, he told me I was playing well. "If only you could handle the ball," he said. "If only *anybody* could handle the ball." He told me to go to early mass and come by in the morning before our game out at St. Leo's and he'd teach me an important move.

My mother had made it to the Holy Trinity game and my parents were now delighted with my success. They planned on driving out to St. Leo's for the game with Sylvie and Andy and Joe, after eleven o'clock mass. When my parents were getting along, my father went to mass with the family. As he said, "Church is church," though he was happy that he didn't have to go if he didn't want.

That Sunday morning I served an early mass, then met Callahan in the gym. He handed me the basketball. "I think that chest is loose enough now," he said. "Let's try putting those powerful legs to use."

He had me shoot a lay-up. He worked on my footing. Then he showed me how to pick the ball up off the dribble, at the beginning of one step, then take the legal extra step-and-a-half off the drive. I took to it immediately. I found I could pick up my dribble on a run near top of the key and fly to the basket.

"Great!" yelled Callahan. "Great! You, at this moment, cannot comprehend what this will do for your game." Now, he said, I could fill the wing on the fast break, and in the half-court game, come out from the corner to take the ball, then shoot or drive the lane. That Sunday afternoon at St. Leo's, the team that had embarrassed us 13–0 in our football opener, we scored eighty points. I led all scorers with twenty-three. After the game Callahan came out and met my parents. As always, he was buoyant and gracious.

"Mr. Rosenthal, Mrs. Rosenthal, I guess you're pretty proud of your boy here," he said.

My father beamed and my mother almost cried. Callahan let me ride home with my family instead of the team. "I told you," my father said in the car. "I told you he'd need you. And when you got your chance, you showed him!"

Indeed, I had. Twenty-three points. And I owed it all to Callahan. He'd given me the opportunity and the time. He made me. And in that moment I'd never been happier in my life.

In the next game, a walk-over at home against St. Jerome's, Callahan started Raymond Luciani instead of Kenny Bruce. It was Raymond's chance to prove what he could do. He played Raymond the whole game. Using my new move to the basket, I scored twenty-four of our seventy-two points. Raymond Luciani went scoreless, missing every shot he took, continually losing the ball out of bounds, and twice at the foul line he threw the ball up and missed the whole rim.

Afterward, amid our jubilation, Raymond sat on the end of locker room bench, his head in his hands, crying loudly. I recalled my misery after we beat St. Paul's in football and felt sorry for him. I put my hand on his shoulder and said, "Come on, you'll do better next time."

Luciani threw my hand from his shoulder and stood. "You replaced me!" he shouted. "You'll see. You'll see what you're in for. He ruined me!" Raymond cried. "The bastard! The bastard! He ruined me!"

Chapter Ten

We ran through the end of our first half schedule winning seven in a row and finishing in a tie for third. St. Pete's won the first half title in a play-off. But in our league, after everybody had played each other once, the slate was wiped clean and we started over. The second half champion met the first half champion for the city title, and it was obvious to a lot of people, as Callahan said, "that Holy Name was once again a force to be reckoned with." To us he was more direct. "Gentlemen," he said, "you will win the second half."

In the interim between halves, Callahan scheduled some games against local junior high schools who only played their eighth graders and second string ninth graders against us, as well as some rural parishes, all of whom we manhandled. It seemed that all of our work against our bigger, stronger alumni had begun to pay off. We grew confident and unintimidated as our win streak ballooned and we looked forward to our second half opener at St. Mark's with tremendous confidence. We would beat them. Then we would go to St. Joe's and win. Then we'd knock off St. Pete's in our gym and after the first three games the second half would be in our pocket.

The only question mark now seemed to be Kenny Bruce. Kenny was funny and popular and I envied him. He loved to turn situations into Smothers Brothers comedy routines. Several girls had crushes on him, including Sally Thomas. He wore his hair in what was called a "Princeton," a kind of crew cut with short bangs which I thought looked ridiculous, but Kenny said that all the college kids were wearing them.

Kenny was sweet and light-hearted, an easy-going Irish kid with few ambitions. His step-brothers were both superb, all-city athletes in both basketball and football. His oldest brother, Davie Kay, had played split-end for Stuben Tech. Kenny's other brother, Danny, was a star on Holy Name's team when Kenny made the varsity in sixth grade. But Kenny, his father's son from an earlier marriage—his mom was dead—had little of his of his step-brothers' intensity and none of their genes.

As basketball season progressed, Kenny grew edgy. He'd already blown a couple games and I worried that my success bothered him like it did Raymond. Once, after he arrived with Callahan for a late practice, I saw him wander off by himself, standing by the exit down the hallway, hesitating there, then staring out into nothing.

"Hey," I said to him. "Come on. We're going to do it."

"Maybe," Kenny said. He shook his head. "I don't know."

"What's not to know? Just get the ball to Huffy or Wooj." I laughed. "Or me."

Kenny turned. His eyes watered and he wiped the tears away with his finger tips. "I don't know if I can keep doing it," he said.

"Yeah," I said, "you can. Come on." I took his elbow.

He yanked it away. "Not basketball," he said. "*It.*" He went out the door. That was the last time he showed for after-supper practice. I thought the line had been drawn between those who endured and those who couldn't, between those who could go into the storage room and take the pain, like me, in order to be transformed, and those who didn't have it.

Kenny and Wooj were with me on the Solemn High Mass Crew, so besides basketball we served mass together almost every day because we worked all the funerals and Holy Name was still a big parish. On some days we served two or three funeral ceremonies and spent most of the day out of school.

Dealing with funerals every day made us cynical and Kenny was still funny, always good for a fart or pun. Sometimes even the priests laughed it up with us a little bit before heading out to send a notorious drunk or adulterer to his eternal reward.

"So why do we bother?" I once said to Fr. Hobart, a big, gentle man who was the Bishop's secretary and who resided at Holy Name.

"Oh," he said, "you never know. In the end, it's our place to pray and God's place to judge." Though he did ask me why I didn't go to communion at every mass.

"It's against the rules," I said. "Sometimes I forget and break the fast. And sometimes I take communion at the first mass I serve, then I can't take it at the others."

Hobart smiled his gentle smile and put his hand under my chin. "Did the apostles fast before Jesus instituted the sacrament at the Last Supper?" he said. "It seems to me they spent the whole time eating." When I didn't say anything he added, "You are like an apostle. Follow your heart. The rules are not for you."

Earlier that year, on the wings of Vatican II, the parishes were told by the Archbishop to begin saying the mass in English, and they were ordered to stop using their big, marble altars and begin saying mass on tables that faced the congregation. The priests and nuns were in a frenzy about what to do, but I sat down over a weekend and worked out a liturgy for both high and low masses, as well as solemn high masses. It was just a matter of moving people around. Hobart quickly employed my liturgy, then took it to our pastor and soon all the priests in the parish used it. Then Hobart showed it to the Archbishop.

Not long after, the Archbishop's mother died and the Cathedral, without yet having redesigned their own altar or worked out a new, English liturgy, moved the huge funeral to Holy Name. I ended up coaching a slew of monsignors and priests on how to participate in the new, high funeral mass in English, and I was the Master of Ceremonies for the Archbishop's burial of his mother, personally directing puzzled old priests around the redesigned sacristy. Afterward, I was a celebrity. Even Huffy Roberts told me, "You're one fuckin' famous altar boy."

Not that I'd ever win the friendship of kids like Huffy, but my status on the basketball team turned much of my unforgivable goodness into something they could ignore. Once the thirteenth man, I was now the team's third highest scorer.

More than my accomplishments on the basketball floor, my mother was thrilled with my status as a diocesan celebrity. One evening after saying the rosary together, as we knelt at the dining room table under the statue of the Blessed Virgin, she asked me, "Chuck, do you still think about becoming a priest?"

"Yes," I said, "sometimes, but I'm kind of involved with basketball now."

"Of course," Helen said. "You're so young."

But in fact, I thought of Herbie Thomas' older sister, Sally, constantly—how her legs slid within the sheer skin of her hose and her breasts pushed against her blouse; I thought of her blue eyes and how the white scarf she wore in church framed her face and held her thick, blonde hair against her cheeks—I thought of her with constant pleasure and guilt, even while serving mass.

Besides, Fr. Hobart's attempt to free me from the constrictions of Catholic conformity, to take me gently into the arms of the faithful elite, instead shook my faith. How could there be different rules? At moments I felt like Lucifer, blessed in light by God, but deep inside sinful and corrupt. Now the right hand of the Archbishop had freed me to abandon the rules and let my heart guide me. My heart was a volcano. My heart didn't care about Jesus. My heart wanted Sally Thomas.

I thought of my father, condemned by the Church, and puzzled over the doom of humanity under Original Sin, the thousands of ignorant, unbaptized or non-Catholic souls sent to hell by the choices of Eve. Sometimes, like Lucifer and like Eve, I wondered why God so wished to protect His power that He would condemn forever those who sought knowledge. He seemed frightened and unforgiving. And I fell into Calvin's dilemma of reconciling free will with God's omniscience.

One night after an after-supper workout, Callahan drove me home. When he parked in front of my house he said, "You sniffle all the time."

"Sinuses," I said. I took it for granted. I always had headaches. My chest hurt. For a while, Helen took me to a specialist who tortured my nostrils and throat with acidic cotton packs, steam guns and tubes, trying to get me to gag up phlegm.

"Your sinuses are why you start so slow," he said. "Come here, put your head on my leg. I want to check something."

He had me put my head on his lap while he massaged the sinus cavities in my cheeks and forehead. Inside the dry heat of the puttering car, the blackness outside, I lay with my head on my coach's lap. As he ran his fingers into my face bones, despite the pain I felt the mucous drain into my throat. It worked. It always worked. It took away my headaches and for a night allowed me to breathe. Sometimes, knowing he'd be doing it, we'd drive to McDonald's for some burgers and fries, and a shake that I'd save and drink after his sinus therapy, to settle my stomach. I loved those trips because my parents never took the family out. He let me eat all I wanted. Callahan and I began to talk then, about things besides basketball.

He was thirty, though when he asked me to guess his age I said, "Fifty," which made him roar with laughter. He was born and raised in a small oil town below Toledo, but came south to attend Stuben College. That's when he started coaching, though in high school he never played beyond J.V. He spent a year coaching grade school basketball at Cathedral Grade School before coming to Holy Name for the first time. More remarkable than his basketball success were his championships in football. As he'd said, his last team at Holy Name went unscored upon as well as undefeated.

Callahan went to Ohio U. for his M.A. in history and coached J.V. high school basketball at a Catholic prep in Athens. Teaching and coaching in Cleveland he got interested in physical therapy. He said he was fascinated with the human body. Now he was back in Stuben, teaching at St. Mary's College while summers he pursued his Ph.D. at Ohio State.

It was after a Friday night workout, on the way into the parking lot at McDonald's, when he asked me how many hamburgers I wanted and I told him I couldn't eat meat because it was Friday.

He laughed. "Really?" he said.

"No," I said. "Do you?"

He laughed again. "I suppose you believe that the devil's next to you, trying to get you to do it."

"Maybe," I said. "Maybe he is."

"And your guardian angel?"

I saw I was being baited, so I didn't say anything.

We went in and he let me get my fish sandwich, but back in the car he asked me, "Do you believe in Noah's Ark?"

"Sure," I said. "Why not? It's in the Bible." I hadn't really noticed till that moment that he was eating a cheeseburger.

"You believe that Noah gathered two of every animal in the world and put them on a boat," he said.

"It was a miracle," I said.

He nodded. "God needed Noah to do that. He couldn't have done it Himself. Just saved the good people and the animals." He paused. "He killed a lot of innocent animals," Callahan said, and smirked.

Maybe it would have happened without Callahan. Likely, some-time. I don't know. But I was only thirteen. Callahan was the man I admired and the only person whose respect I craved. In an in-stant, my house of cards fell. I looked out of the car and into the night, the hiss of automobiles on the pavement, their yellow head-lights streaming and red tail lights streaking the dark; the neon lights from businesses shining onto the sidewalks and the street lights reflecting on the wet, black street under a gentle, falling snow. How easy it was to travel on a dark, cold, winter night with the warm power of an engine under a cascade of artificial light. I looked at Callahan. "Can I have a cheeseburger?" I said.

"They're in the bag," he said. "Get one yourself."

Only a few days later I pulled a muscle in my inner thigh. The usual team treatment for muscle injuries was to rub the injured area with some kind of liniment, Red Hot Horse Liniment or Atomic Balm, and then, contrary to the directions, wrap it in an Ace Bandage. The burning was often excruciating, but if it didn't cure the injury, at least it distracted you enough until you warmed up the muscle during play. It was Huffy Robert's clever use of muscle liniment which convinced me to stop wearing a jock strap. He filled up Herbie's strap with Atomic Balm before one practice and Herbie went through the roof. He made it through the whole workout, but spent a night in the shower screaming.

With our second half opener at St. Mark's on the horizon, I limped through practice and into my after-supper workout before Callahan stopped me and told me to shower up. "Come on," he said. "Let's go to my place and fix that."

I dressed and we drove to his apartment, a second story flat where he lived with his cousin, Bernard, a navy reservist. The house was only a few blocks east of mine. We walked up the steps at the side of the house and entered by way of the kitchen, a tiny living room with a couch and a TV sat off to the left. Straight ahead was Callahan's bedroom. Bernard's room, not visible from the kitchen, was only accessible through Callahan's. I didn't notice much. Callahan's bed was in the far right corner of the small room. A print of a mounted Indian running down a buffalo hung on the wall over the bed.

Callahan told me to go into his bedroom and take off my pants. To do that I had to take my shoes off, too. He came in and sat on the bed in front of me and told me to face him. He put his fingers into the muscle of my inner thigh. "Hamstring," he said. "Take off your underwear."

I hesitated.

He looked up at me. "Take off your underwear, Mr. Rosenthal," Callahan said. "What's the matter?"

I stuttered at him. He'd already held my nuts while spanking me, but that was in the storage room. This was his bedroom. "My mother told me never to let anyone touch me there," I whispered.

"What!" screamed Callahan. He pushed me away from him, almost knocking me down. "What are you saying?" He glared at me. "Do you know what you're saying?"

I looked at the floor. I stuttered again. "I'm just saying what my mother said to me," I said. I was thirteen. I didn't know anything.

But already Callahan was in a rage in front of me. "I will never be accused of that! I won't take that from you *or* your mother!" he screamed. He threw my pants at me. "Get out of here!" he yelled. "Keep your damn thigh injury. Get off the team! If that's what you think, I never want to see you again!"

I struggled into my pants as I backed up against the kitchen door. I didn't even know what I'd really said, but now, in a sentence, I'd blown my whole life. I'd blown everything.

"I'm sorry," I said. "I don't know what she meant."

He watched me. He saw me eyeing my shoes which were sitting underneath him.

"Do you want that leg taken care of?" he said.

"Yes," I said. "Yes, sir."

"Come here," he said.

And slowly I came forward.

"Take off your pants and your underwear."

Warily, I did.

"Your shirt will get in the way," he said. "Take it off."

I took my shirt off, too. Thinking back, it's hard to find the threshold of surrender, because I had given myself up to Callahan in a hundred ways a hundred times before. But in that moment I left the side of my mother, I left her world and the Motherhood of the Church; I let go of my father's hand and entered puberty, a manhood of my own. Humble and penitent, a blushing, naked boy, I stood in front of Dan Callahan, the replacement of the God I'd just abandoned.

Chapter Eleven

Callahan fixed my hamstring. It was a painful process, but miraculous, too. He got out a book and showed me illustrations of the musculature of the human thigh and how one of my muscles was lying on top of another, popped out of alignment by strain. What he did was first relax the area, loosening the muscles around the pulled one, then push the muscle back into place. He applied heat and wrapped it for the night. Once in, more likely than not, it would hold.

It took a long time and I cried some. He told me to shut up or he'd stop. When he was done he applied Atomic Balm and wrapped the leg. "There's a faster, less painful way to do that, to loosen you," he said.

"How?"

"Well," he shrugged. "Anyway, you're really tight. Your muscles are thick and as hard as bricks. I don't know if you'll ever be loose enough to play basketball on a higher level."

I didn't say anything.

"Do you want to play in high school?" Callahan asked me. I hesitated again and he said, "Put on your pants. Get dressed. I get no pleasure out of looking at naked kids."

I got my underwear and pants. "I just want to beat St. Mark's," I said.

"Me too, Mr. Rosenthal," he said. "Me too. But do you want to know something? Win or lose, in a couple years no one will remember."

It was a Hobart moment, but then I missed it. Callahan loved the futility of human effort. In the next few years he made me memorize all of the American Presidents, learn each of the American states and their capitals, and be able to draw a regional map of every area of the world including every country, every capital, and the resources, industry, agriculture, and demographics of each nation. He taught me that life was frail, fame fleeting, that in the human heart lay the denizens of short-sighted greed, as well as the glory of altruism. That it all came to naught, meant nothing. That it came at all, meant everything.

He turned to me. "But if we beat St. Mark's, you boys are going to win the second half title. I'd planned for the second half all along." He hesitated a moment as I finished dressing. "What do you know about sex, Mr. Rosenthal?" he said.

"You know," I said shyly. "Just what everybody knows."

"Which is what?"

Well, the answer was absolutely nothing.

"Sit down," he said and got out another book, this one the *Time-Life* volume on Human Sexuality. He opened the book. Using the pictures and illustrations he showed me the male sexual organs and the female. He explained sexual intercourse, sperm, eggs, conception. When he was done he said, "Any questions?"

"Why would anyone do it?" I asked.

He laughed loudly. "You're a funny kid," Callahan said. "You say the wildest things." He got up. "Do you have a girlfriend?" he asked.

"I like Herbie's sister, Sally," I said.

"Does she like you?"

"She likes Kenny," I said.

"The story of the world, Mr. Rosenthal," said Callahan. "The story of the world." He tousled my hair. Since that night in the hallway before the St. Pete's game, when he'd momentarily put his arm around my shoulder, it was the first time he touched me with any affection. "With your looks you'll have a hundred Sally Thomas's, Mr. Rosenthal," Dan Callahan said. "A hundred. Now let's get you home."

We took dead aim on St. Mark's. Their gym, a little, green tiled cafeteria band box, had only a few rows of folding chairs set up on the sidelines, not even enough seats to hold our fans, let alone theirs. And the place rocked from the start. It was a huge game, but we were a changed team and no one doubted that this time we would win.

Callahan put us in a triangle-and-two defense, three boys playing a zone and two man-to-man on their star guard and center, and it troubled them the whole first half. Up by six at half-time, Callahan was calm and matter-of-fact in the locker room. We'd open the third quarter in a man-to-man, just to keep them off balance. It worked and at the end of three periods we led by ten.

Callahan never advocated freezing the ball to protect a lead. He felt grade school players would just throw the ball away. But he did drop us into a three-two zone for the fourth quarter, to slow the pace. St. Mark's came out pressing in a full-court man-to-man and we broke it, but finally our nerves began to fray. We tightened up and began missing shots. When Callahan called time out with two minutes left, we had the ball and still led by six, 40–34.

"Go back to the man-to-man," he said. "Be aggressive. It's your game." He stood in the middle of the huddle, chopping with his thin hand for emphasis. "They're beaten. It would take a miracle to beat you. A miracle! Stay calm. Drive to the basket. Hit your foul shots. Play defense. Play your game."

When Kenny Bruce brought the ball down the court St. Mark's had switched to a half court zone trap. Kenny panicked and was stripped by their point guard who drove the length of the court and scored. "Give the ball to Huffy!" yelled Callahan, and Kenny passed the ball into Huffy Roberts who dribbled down the wing, broke the trap, and hit Kenny slicing down the middle all alone. Kenny Bruce took the pass on the fly, stretched to the hoop, and blew the lay-up. St. Mark's rebounded and raced down the floor. After two or three passes, their big center scored inside and our lead was cut to 40–38.

With less than a minute left we brought the ball down the floor. Though I had ten points and several rebounds, I was too frightened to shoot, and so were Kenny and Herbie, but thank God neither Huffy nor Wooj were bright enough to fear failure. Huffy broke the press again and hit Wooj in the pivot. The Wooj faced the basket, shot, and scored. With under thirty seconds left we led 42–38 and we were jumping and cheering on the floor. St. Mark's hurried the ball down the court, but we all collapsed down low on their center. He managed a feeble pass out to the wing with less than ten seconds left. Their star guard hit a jumper. But there were only about six seconds left. Callahan was yelling not to touch the ball at all, to let the clock run out, but no one heard. The Wooj took the ball out of bounds and passed it to Kenny Bruce who was fouled with four seconds to go.

We were out of time outs, but if Kenny hit the first foul shot of the one-and-one, the game was over. And even if he missed, there wasn't enough time for St. Mark's to get the ball down the floor and shoot, even with a home-court clock. Callahan sent the team manager down to the scorer's table to watch the clock keeper. Kenny Bruce went to the line, shivering. Having just missed a game-winning lay-up, this foul shot was his chance to be a hero, his chance to put the game away, to launch us on our ride to the title, to confirm the athletic heritage that he inherited from his family. He raised the ball weakly, released, and missed.

In the scramble for the rebound Callahan screamed, "Turn on the clock! Turn on the clock!" The ball went to the floor and was finally retrieved by St. Mark's big man on the baseline who began to dribble up court. The game should have been long over, but when you play away from home, sometimes you have to play a little longer. The kid reached half court and launched a wild, lunging shot as the buzzer finally sounded. The ball bounded off the bank board and our fans rushed the floor, hugging us, until we finally noticed the referee blowing his whistle furiously at center court. He'd called a foul on Kenny Bruce for hacking in the act of shooting. As our stunned fans cleared the floor, St. Mark's center went to the line, standing alone in the silent gym, the clock run out.

Callahan was furious with everyone: the clock keeper, our manager, the referee, but most of all Kenny Bruce. He turned to Kenny, who stood faint and quaking in front of him, and growled, "You fouled a man at half court with no time on the clock? You fouled a man taking a half-court shot?" Then he muttered to himself. "It's too much pressure. A kid can't hit two shots like that." But he did. He coolly canned both free throws and we were in overtime.

The next few minutes were the defining moments of our season. Callahan tried to calm us. We'd beaten them for four quarters, we could beat them again. We went back to the zone, but St. Mark's scored off the opening tip. When they dropped into a zone themselves, Kenny Bruce brought the ball slowly up the floor. They jumped out on him, stripped the ball, and went down and scored. Down by four now, Kenny brought the ball up again, dribbling slowly. It was then that I noticed he was crying. He stopped before the half court line and lifted the ball to his waist, his face cracking and the tears now pouring from his eyes. Almost gently, the St. Mark's defender took the ball from him and dribbled down the floor, while at center court, in front of six hundred silent fans, Kenny Bruce fell to his knees, collapsed, and wept.

Chapter Twelve

The crushing defeat at St. Mark's ended our season. A number of years later, during a party in his living room with Holy Name alumni, Callahan laughed about it. He turned to me and said, "You kids were that close." He made an inch between his thumb and index finger. "That close from the miracle." Then he spread his arms out downward from his chair, opened his hands and shook his head. "I've never seen anybody collapse like that. Never! I looked up and thought, My God, my point guard is crying! My point guard is crying!" Then he shook his head again. "What a total collapse. Bruce never had what it took to amount to anything. Where is he now? Divorced. Uneducated. A nothing."

In our next game, which began by Kenny racing with the opening tip to the wrong basket, missing the lay-up only to have Wooj tip it in, St. Joe's blew us out by seventeen. Before the game Callahan threatened to start playing the seventh graders if we lost, and afterward he was true to his word. He used them predominantly in our next loss, an overtime defeat at home to St. Pete's, and in two more one point losses. Though we smacked St. Dominic's again and finished with four wins against crummy teams, the season was a disaster. At 18–11 we were the worst team in the history of Holy Name basketball. At the end of the year our girls' team, which went undefeated, challenged us to a game. Kenny and I were all for it. Callahan would have none of it. For them it was win-win, he said, and for us lose-lose.

One of the highlights of the year was our season-ending, week-end trip to Cleveland where we played a rematch against St. Augustine's on a high school floor and stayed overnight in a hotel. Callahan gave the first half to the eighth graders and at half-time we led by two and I had fourteen points. But in the second half he leaned on the seventh graders again and took the defeat. Afterward he was casual and friendly, as if the game meant nothing. We visited the Planetarium and the Museum of Natural History. I wanted to be an astronomer and Kenny wanted to be a paleontologist. At the planetarium I saw my first star show and the Museum had a great mummy collection. Kenny and I had a blast. Cleveland seemed an enormous metropolis of dreams.

Raymond Luciani, Wooj, Kenny, and I stayed in the same room. Callahan stayed in the suite next door. The four of us were thinking about heading down to the indoor pool and were dancing around naked, swinging our swim suits in the air and singing to The Association's "Along Comes Mary" on the radio. Suddenly Callahan opened the suite door. We fell silent. Dan Callahan shook his head. "Kids," he said. Then he pointed to Raymond. "Okay, Mr. Luciani, you first." Raymond wrapped a towel around himself. Head down, he followed Callahan into his room. The three of us shrugged and headed for the pool. Kenny got the call when we got back and Raymond, Wooj and I sat quietly for a minute. That was all. I was third that night, and then Wooj.

I don't know what went on with those other kids. We never spoke of it. For me, aside from the painful chest pounding which had almost become commonplace, Callahan now worked on elongating the muscles in my thighs. He worked in his jockey-shorts, T-shirt, and socks. I was naked. One exercise that I feared and hated was when he had me lie on my back while he placed himself between my thighs and spread them out with his elbows. It always made me cry and left me panting and begging him to stop. I thought that it was the most painful thing I'd ever felt, but it wouldn't be.

After spreading my legs, Callahan held me close to him, chest to chest, and pressed into my thighs with his fingers, digging them into my muscles. It hurt, but as he said, it was the price of my having any chance at a future in basketball, and compared to the thigh spreading it was a relief. Then he probed my forehead for a while, clearing my sinuses. Sometimes, afterward, we wrestled, though he cheated if I got an advantage, tugging me away by pulling my hair or briefly grabbing my testicles. That was his rule. He was the adult. He got to cheat.

Afterward we lay together and talked. I always felt uncomfortable lying next to him, but if I tried to move away he'd grab my hair and say, "Trying to get away, are you, Mr. Rosenthal?" and jokingly pull me back down. It was man stuff. Men and boys. Like the ancient Greeks.

That night in Cleveland he told me that I played a great first half. He said that the other coach didn't even remember me from the last time we played and thought I was a ringer.

"Why didn't you let me play more in the second half?" I said.

"When you got in, I just used you as a decoy anyway," he said. "I didn't think it would work as well if you knew. I was trying to open things up for Huffy, but it failed, so I pulled you."

"I don't get it," I said.

"What do you mean, you 'don't get it'?"

"What if I would have scored thirty? We might have won."

"Players of your caliber seldom put together two great halves in a row, Mr. Rosenthal," Callahan said. "I played the odds. And for the future, I played the seventh graders. Besides, there's nothing for you to get. You're young. There's a lot you don't get."

It was true, there was too much I didn't get. How could I understand that I depended on him for everything? How I thought of him constantly. How much he dominated my life. I was a thirteen year old boy. I was in love with him. And that was too much for me to understand.

Chapter Thirteen

When the basketball season ended Callahan immediately organized an intramural program for the fifth through eighth grades, his in-school scouting program. He started a fifth-sixth grade junior varsity team and hired an old St. Pete's star, Neal O'Donnel, to coach them, as well as the seventh grade supplemental team. All year Callahan opened the gym up to his alumni and supervised alumni scrimmages every day in which he worked his varsity players into the competition. The year after my eighth grade season, he staged a three-on-three league. He hand-picked each team which carried one ninth grade alumnus, and one graduating eighth grader or seventh grade letterman, and one sixth or seventh grader. That spring I stopped shooting the ball from my chest and began lifting it off my right shoulder. Though unorthodox, it was deadly. I became a vicious competitor. To everyone's surprise, my team won the title and I led the league in scoring.

One night after an individual workout, just a few days before the annual sports awards banquet, Callahan met me outside the locker room. His put his arm over my shoulder as we walked down the hall.

"Who would you say was the most valuable player on the basketball team?" Callahan asked.

"Wooj," I said.

"And football?"

"Huffy."

"You're an honest man, Mr. Rosenthal," Callahan said. "A remarkably honest young man. How about an eighth grader?"

"Me," I said. "Me and Huffy had all the touchdowns till the last game."

"Why not Kenny?" Callahan said.

"Kenny?" I said. "He wasn't any good." I was not too young to see the ironies. In sixth grade, Kenny had made varsity in basketball instead of me. Now Callahan was asking me to sacrifice the MVP trophy to my friend. I looked at Callahan. "I'm better than Kenny at everything now," I said. "That's the reason you want to give him the MVP trophy."

"Kenny Bruce will never get another award in his life," Callahan said. "Let him have this one. I'll give you a trophy for MVP of the three-on-three league."

But I didn't give up. I was more intimate with him now, and though I feared him, still, I pressed him. "You tell *me* that I might not have a future," I said.

Callahan smirked and almost winced. "Is that so, Mr. Rosenthal?" he said. "Is that so? I guess sometimes, Mr. Rosenthal, I underestimate you."

It was the first time that I really felt he had.

That spring, at one of a series of graduation parties, I danced with a lot of girls who liked me and none of whom I wanted. At each occasion I ended up staring across the room at Sally Thomas as she flirted in front of Kenny, who clowned about. Her hands moved in front of her, trying to touch him almost against her will. She'd coax him into a fast dance, the Swim or the Monkey, but during a slow dance he'd disappear. And I'd watch the points of her breasts against her blouse, the tilt of her ankles in her heels, the shine of her nylons over her slender calves, her blonde hair cascading over her shoulders, her blue eyes.

Then one Friday night when there were two parties, I showed up late and found Sally there and no Kenny. She brooded so sadly I almost cried. I danced with the hostess, an old nemesis of mine, the smartest girl in the class. She heckled me constantly, which I'd finally come to understand meant that she was attracted to me. Then a phone call came in from the other party over at Janice Lewski's. Girls poured out of the kitchen with the buzz. Kenny Bruce was there. Janice had finally nailed him. She and Kenny Bruce were going steady.

As I stood against the wall, Sally Thomas walked out of the kitchen and stood in front of me. I quaked.

"Would you like to dance with me?" she said. She smiled a little and lowered her eyes shyly.

"Really?" I said.

She shrugged. We were just kids. "You're my second choice," she said to me. "I'd be stupid to lose you both."

That night I danced a slow dance with a girl for the first time. My penis got so hard that it frightened me. Before long, we kissed. Sally Thomas was mine.

Early in the summer, after school had let out, Callahan planned a trip to Washington D.C. and told Kenny, Wooj, and me that if we got our parents' permission, he'd drive us down there with him. We'd visit the battlefield at Gettysburg on the way and then stay at a motel with a pool in D.C. Though Callahan hired a guide in Gettysburg, a grizzly old man full of stories and mythology, Callahan himself knew the battlefields as well, and knew more facts. We visited the 360 degree diorama show and the lighted battle map, then went out for a tour of the battlefield: Big Round Top, Little Round Top, the Devil's Den, Cemetery Ridge.

Finally, we stood at the top of the hill where General Mead drew up the Union line of defense. We stared down across the long field from where Lee sent Picket and the Army of Northern Virginia up the slope to break the Union center. Near the grove of trees where the Confederacy briefly breached the Union line before being thrown back, Callahan narrated the fatal charge: the lines of men in nut brown and gray advancing briskly up the hill, the sun glistening off their bayonets as they marched magnificently forward toward the Yankee guns filled with the shrapnel which would cut down a thousand young men in a single barrage. The Rebel Yell. The deafening roar of musket fire and cannon. The Yankees chanting, "Fredricksburg! Fredricksburg!" where they themselves had last charged and been slaughtered. You could still find bullets on that hill. The museum was filled with diaries and notes sketched out to loved ones as men lay in the field, badly wounded, near dead.

"Would you be so brave, gentlemen?" Callahan said to us. "Ask yourselves, would you be so brave?"

That night, in his room, in his bed, I felt I was brave enough. Callahan added a twist to the tightening-loosening therapy. After stretching my thighs, something which I'd learned to endure in silence, he took hold of my testicles and shifted them softly in his palm. He gripped the right testicle and began to squeeze. The pain wracked me, shooting through my groin, into my abdomen and chest and down my leg; my groin felt as if it would burst. When he released, I quivered and cried with nausea and relief, but quickly he moved to the other testicle. I lurched, my stomach flying upward above my arched back. Every part of me surged into cramps. I had never felt such pain. He did it three times on each testicle. To muffle my screams, he covered my mouth with his own.

In Washington, Callahan turned us loose in the Smithsonian, took us to Arlington National Cemetery and Mount Vernon. In the cool of night we visited the Jefferson Memorial, the Lincoln Memorial, and climbed the Washington Monument. Now Callahan lectured us about the American Revolution and told us the biographies of Washington, John Adams, Hamilton, and Burr, though most of all, Jefferson, whom he greatly admired.

On our last day we toured the White House, hoping to see Lyndon Johnson or his beagles, and went inside the Capital building as Callahan explained how the British burned Washington D.C. during the War of 1812. That night we sat before the Capital, its lit dome white against the black sky, the American flag waving in the light breeze under the lights, and Callahan explained the three branches of government, the battle over states' rights at the Constitutional Convention, the compromises which made American democracy the greatest government on earth, the glory of the American tripartite balance of power: executive, judicial, and legislative.

"The great American experiment has produced the greatest, most powerful nation in the world. The greatest nation this world has ever known!" Callahan exclaimed. "Look at what happened when Kennedy was assassinated. In any other nation of the world, such an abrupt tragedy would have produced a crisis in the transfer of power. Say what you will about the American people, gentlemen, in a world of chaos and turmoil, *we* are stable. Our government is greater than any one man."

He talked of how the United States twice saved Europe, in both World War One and World War Two, and both times received their ingratitude. He talked of the American generosity of rebuilding Germany and Japan. "No nation on earth has ever been so powerful, so rich, and so generous." Yet, he said, many times our democracy came close to falling apart. He spoke of the early troubles after the Revolution and reminded us of Gettysburg and the Civil War. "But God loves fools, drunkards, and the United States of America, gentlemen. God loves fools, drunkards, and the United States."

And that night, as every night in Washington, he took us one by one out of our room. Hundreds of boys passed through Callahan's hands the same way and went on to become college basketball stars and coaches, judges, congressmen, senators, navy captains, mayors. As he told me, he was doing all he could with the imperfect body in front of him to turn it into the body of a basketball player. He took the time out of his life to do it for us. He helped boys achieve their dreams.

Just before graduating from Holy Name, I served my last Solemn High Ceremony. I was the Master of Ceremonies for my own Confirmation and took Augustine as my Confirmation name because of his intellectual brilliance. At the end of the ceremony, as each of my classmates came forth and the Bishop passed us into Christian adulthood, I stood at his left hand. When he was done, he confirmed the mass crew, turning, at the very last, to me.

By then Callahan had taken away my Edgar Ryce Burroughs and given me *Catcher in the Rye*, *Lord of the Flies*, and *A Separate Peace*. If I could not remember the author's name when he quizzed me, he spelled it out on my ass. I read biographies of Socrates, Plato, Pericles, Hannibal, and Caesar. Callahan pointed out the Greek penchant for young boys. He remarked that Julius Caesar was bisexual. He gave me an historical biography of Christ, as well, a book which exposed the miracles as myths and explained how the gospels could not have been written by contemporaries of Christ. When the Bishop finally turned to me and lay his hands on my head to commit my life to the Catholic Church, it was already too late. I'd been an atheist for quite some time.

Chapter Fourteen

⸺⸺⸺

In the middle of summer, 1965, Dan Callahan left Stuben for Columbus to pursue courses in English history at Ohio State and conduct research for his doctoral dissertation. He wrote me long letters about basketball and patriotism and I wrote him back. He complained bitterly about a group of people he called the Vietniks who opposed the American intervention in Vietnam. He found them dirty, cowardly, and disgusting.

Though I'd joined the YMCA and often played basketball there both mornings and evenings, Callahan made it clear to me how little progress I could make on my own. I could hone skills he'd taught me, but I would not get better without his personal coaching, and my body would never develop without his therapy and training. He sent me a plane ticket to fly to Columbus in August to join him during his last week of school. Afterward we would fly to New York City to see the World's Fair. My parents were delighted by the opportunity this gave me, though my siblings, particularly my older sister, Aubrey, were jealous.

In the meantime, June and July seemed months of endless joy. Sally, now my first girlfriend, had a best friend, Diane, who began dating a neighbor of mine, Tommy Cale, and Tommy and I spent the summer making the two mile walk through the downtown to the Public Pier to catch the ferry to the river beach where we'd meet Sally and Diane. I had my first transistor radio and we listened to the Beatles and Stones and a hundred other Mercy Beat bands from the British invasion or, tuning into CKLW from beyond Lake Erie in Windsor, Canada and Detroit, we grooved to Motown; the Temptations, Gladys Knight and the Pips, the Four Tops. Sneaking off behind the trees, lying down on a blanket and covering ourselves with beach towels, Sally and I necked and petted to Barbara Mason's "But I'm Ready to Learn."

In the evenings, after I'd get done working out, I walked over to Tommy's house—he was an only child—and we listened to the Beatles and Stones on his stereo while we planned sleep-outs on the same night as Sally and Diane. Waiting until after one a.m., we slipped out of the tent and trekked the shadows of back streets to Sally's or Diane's backyard. Usually Diane and Tommy took a walk and left me and Sally in the tent. There, stripped to our underwear, we touched each other's lips, our ears, tongues, breasts, everything but our private parts, and even those fragile organs kissed beneath the thin membrane of cotton and nylon which separated them. "I love you," I told her. And she loved me, too. The touch of Sally's hand thrilled me. We were thirteen.

In early August I kissed Sally good-bye and kissed my mother, Helen, good-bye and shook my father, Sam's, hand and got on my first airplane, a two-engine Mohawk Airline "puddle jumper," as Sam called it, to Cleveland, then Columbus. Flying for the first time, and by myself, I was astounded by the spreading landscape of patched farmland, the wide, blue lake and pure, white clouds, though during the puddle jump to Columbus a storm came up and then the airport at Columbus fogged in. We circled Columbus, the plane shuddering in the lightning and clouds, before the pilot finally flew us to Cincinnati where a Mohawk agent put me in a car that drove me to Columbus Airport. Long after midnight, Callahan met me. He said he'd never seen anybody look more forlorn. I was tired and the airline had lost my bag. Callahan drove me to the campus, showed me my little room in an old, stone dormitory and let me go right to sleep. That night, though I'd never had a French class, I dreamt that Sally sat next to me as I cheated from her on a French test. It gave me my first wet dream. I didn't know why, but I was afraid to tell Callahan who after that evening brought me to his room for therapy every night.

In Columbus, while Callahan attended class, I spent my time playing basketball at the gym, swimming in a local water hole and wandering around the campus. I spent time in the book store and the library, sat in on philosophy classes, and at a little coffeehouse I ordered hot, spiced apple juice and listened to the Beatniks and Vietniks recite anti-war poetry and read stories about having all kinds of sex. Back then someone had died and left a large endowment to the school on the provision that the administration give the run of the campus to dogs. There were dogs everywhere, even in the eating halls, and with a little food I could usually find some mutt to share my day.

Later in the visit I took Callahan to the coffeehouse. A man with a short beard read a story about two women making love to each other. Callahan dragged me out of there during the applause. "That was sickening," he said. He must have figured I had too much unsupervised time because the next day he introduced me to a young woman, Annette, who he said was his girlfriend, and now I went swimming with her, though without telling him we sometimes went to the coffeehouse. I didn't think it odd that she spent her days with me and I spent my nights with him. Callahan's room had a bathroom, rugs, a small heater, a refrigerator, and a radio. Mine was small and cold. It didn't have a toilet or even a water faucet. I had no money but what he gave me, a dollar here and there.

On the evening of our last night in Columbus, Dan asked me to show him the swimming hole.

"You've never been there?"

"I'm pretty busy," he said.

We made the winding drive down to the stream and parked in the little hollow where everyone parked. There were no cars there now. Dusk was falling. The sound of the stream rushed through the trees.

"Let's go down," he said.

There was no one there. The dark was falling and in the gray air the foam from the little waterfall above the swimming hole looked cloud-white, the water black.

"I hear you're a pretty good swimmer," Dan said. "Let's see."

"It's cold," I said.

"You swim during the day," said Callahan.

"There's sun during the day," I said.

"Just across and back," he said. "I just want to see something."

It was about fifteen yards across the hole, not far. I took off my socks and shoes, slipped out of my jeans and shirt.

"Jockey's, too," said Callahan. "No sense getting them wet."

It wasn't like he hadn't seen me naked before, but there was a kind of inner-ness to the hotel rooms, the dorm rooms, the storage room, an implicit contract to the privacy of the work we had to do. "It's public," I said to him.

"There's no one here," he said. "I mean, you certainly shouldn't if you're afraid."

I stripped off my shorts and quickly plunged into the icy, black stream. It was extremely cold, but within minutes I was used to it and after swimming across and back, dove under and came up beneath the falls, sitting in the air pocket behind the sheet of white, watching Callahan through the opaque gush, into the dusk. I scooted out, took a dive from the diving ledge above the water hole. Finally I came up in front of him, suddenly shivering enormously in the cold.

"Cold?" he said.

"Freezing."

"Come here." He took off his jacket and put it over my shoulders, then sat down, pulling my back to his chest, hugging me there, his face in my hair, his nose behind my ear, his warm breath on my neck. I felt uncomfortable, even in the dark, even alone, out in public, being hugged by a man; but I was warm now, and he was Dan Callahan.

"Is that better?" he whispered. "Yes," he said, "that's better."

I told myself that I did not feel the hardening of his erection against my back.

Afterward, Callahan and I met Annette for dinner. I'd spent the summer working on a reading list of plays that Callahan had given me—*Oedipus*, *Hamlet*, *The Death of a Salesman*, *A Long Day's Journey Into Night*, *The Flies*, *No Exit*—earlier in the visit Callahan had taken me to a production of Sartre's *No Exit* and the night before we'd just attended Becket's *End Game*. Feeling literary and sophisticated, I told Annette about the story we'd heard in the coffeehouse about two women making love to each other. I couldn't remember the name for what the women were called and said they were "Elizabethans" instead of lesbians. Over that, both Callahan and Annette really cracked up.

"You're embarrassed, Mr. Rosenthal," laughed Callahan from across the table. "You should be. Remember, hell is other people."

The next day Callahan and I caught another puddle jumper to Cleveland and he got air sick and puked the whole way. It was the first time I saw him weak or vulnerable, and in the Cleveland airport, when he balked at getting on the plane for New York, I kidded him about it. "You'll pay for that, Mr. Rosenthal," he said. He wagged his finger jokingly. "There's no escape. You'll pay." But the flight to JFK was a jet, my first jet ride; it was extremely smooth and Callahan didn't puke. In New York we took a helicopter to LaGuardia, another first for me. We stayed at the Roosevelt, in the center of Manhattan and Callahan took me to 42nd Street at 3 a.m. so I could see the city that never slept. He sent me across the street, alone, to get us some pizza, and in seconds a man was upon me, offering me food and money. I fled back to Callahan, across the street. Back to safety.

"Well," said Dan Callahan when I got back. "A lesson learned."

That night he added a new twist to my physical therapy. Though he kept on with the squeezing of my testicles, which always left me sobbing in his arms, instead of first stretching my thighs he said I could opt for getting an erection.

"How would I do that?" I said.

He shrugged and put his hand on my penis, working it a little, and in seconds I was hard. The tightening of my lower stomach, as I responded to his working my penis, was supposed to recapitulate the cramping and stretching of the muscles in my groin. He didn't let me come. When he was done he finished by squeezing my testicles, and when he was finished with them, after quieting my screams with his mouth, he left his mouth on mine. He said it was important for my sinus condition that I get heat, and pressing against me, he held me until he fell asleep and I could push away.

The next day he took me to a movie. A black and white French film about a man who had just been released from jail. He'd been convicted of raping a teen-ager who had misrepresented her age. Now, out of jail and determined to go straight, against his better judgment he lets a young girl befriend him. The two of them spend leisurely, innocent afternoons together and he educates her. But then, just as some of the local people find out about his past, as well as discover his liaisons with the child, the girl turns up missing. The town people corner the innocent man in an old shack where he sometimes met the child. They murder him before the girl shows up and declares his innocence.

"What did you think?" said Callahan after the movie.

"He should have stayed away from the girl," I said.

"But he didn't do anything wrong," said Callahan. "He never did." He looked at me. "Ordinary people jump to conclusions. They never understand. That's why it's better if they don't know. I'm talking about the white lie, Mr. Rosenthal. The noble white lie. Sometimes you must lie to people for their own good. And for *your* own good. Sometimes it is the job of great men to protect people from themselves."

"He could have avoided the problem just by staying away from the girl," I said.

"She was his only friend," said Callahan.

"He ended up dead," I said. "He could have just been lonely, but he ended up dead."

"Some things are worse than death, Mr. Rosenthal. I hope you never find out." He tousled my hair. "Loyalty, Mr. Rosenthal, is the greatest virtue. Betrayal the lowest vice. To avoid betrayal, a lie is nothing."

He loved movies, and soon he took me to see *Becket*, *A Man for All Seasons*, *My Fair Lady*, and *The Prime of Miss Jean Brodie*. I read the plays or accompanying novels, as well, though when he discovered me reading Golding's *Boys and Girls Together*, he ripped it from my hands and threw it away. I resented him for it and wondered what was in the novel that I wasn't supposed to know.

"Am I your finest student?" I asked Callahan there in New York.

"Far from it, Mr. Rosenthal," said Callahan. "Thank God. Far from it. You are a B-plus mind with a B-plus body."

"Not even an A-minus?" I said.

"You're idiosyncratic," said Callahan. "More stubborn than brilliant. You're not very analytical. You lack discipline and rigor. But we're trying to give you those. Build them."

I was hurt. I was special in that he had chosen me, for my unevenness, for my flashes of oddity that the world would never appreciate without his tutelage and honing. He would shape me into something acceptable. I was a boy from a large, poor family. I had nothing, deserved little, and wanted everything. I was a Catholic boy, raised to respect authority and accept guilt. *Mea culpa. Mea culpa. Mea maxima culpa.* And now, both guilty and godless, I was his boy. If great men were brought down by brilliant betrayers, I would never be brilliant enough.

"When we get home," he said, I'll have you read *All the King's Men.*"

"Am I like Sandy, then?" I asked him. "Like in *Miss Jean Brodie?*" The question veiled an increasing preoccupation for me, because in order to accept my relationship with Callahan, I'd begun to identify with girls.

Callahan scratched his chin. "Women are so different," he said. "They're vindictive and less straight forward. 'Hell holds no wrath like a woman's scorn,' Mr. Rosenthal. Sandy takes revenge with her youth. Her body." He hesitated. "Hell, Mr. Rosenthal, you could sleep with anyone you wanted. Why should I care? It wouldn't bother me more or less. But you're like her in that she wasn't Jean Brodie's best."

"Who is?" I said.

"I would never misread you the way Jean Brodie misread Sandy."

"No?" I said.

"No," said Callahan. "You're transparent." Dan Callahan laughed very hard. "Besides," he said, spreading his arms. "What could you possibly betray?"

Chapter Fifteen

At the New York World's Fair, Callahan gave me a twenty and turned me loose. I ran off to see Pepsi's "It's a Small World After All" and GM's "Vision of the Future." I ate my first Belgian Waffle, sat in a Swedish deli and looked at my first open-faced sandwich; I ate my first real steak, a thick *filet mignon*. While sitting in the restaurants Callahan ordered rum and coke and pushed his drink across the table to give me a sip. I liked the thick aftertaste of the rum on the back of my palate and the way the fumes of alcohol moved up behind my nose after the first, sweet syrup of coke hit the tip of my tongue.

On Easter and Christmas and New Year's Eve my mother drank sweet, Mogen David wine mixed with Seven Up. She made a weak mixture of the potion for each of us kids to drink at supper. I always equated it with a sacrament and I'd peel the crust from my white bread, a replica of the host, and eat it with the wine, like the body and blood of Christ.

"Better to have it now, with me," said Callahan, "than have it exist as some mysterious craving."

In no time at all, alcohol was no mystery. When we got back Callahan began letting me drink in his apartment, a pre-mixed concoction called Orange Driver, though soon I was mixing my own vodka and orange juice, and not too long later sneaking it home where things had begun to turn. Helen took me aside one evening and sat me down at the dining room table, under her Blessed Virgin, where we used to say the rosary together.

"Do you want to pray with me?" she asked.

"No," I said.

"I didn't think so," said my mother. "Want to share some Pepsi?"

Sharing Pepsi was a big deal. Though Sam was working now, we still only bought an eight-pack of Pepsi a week, usually rationed out on Friday nights. Helen got a bottle from the pantry, put ice in two glasses and poured.

"I'm a little worried," she said.

"I'm fine," I said.

"Is Callahan Catholic?" said Helen.

"What do you mean?"

"Does he tell you not to go to church?"

"No," I said. "We don't talk about it."

"Do you go?"

"Sure."

"Really?"

"Yes."

"You went in Columbus?"

"I go now," I said. "Now that I'm back." This was somewhat true. I left the house on Sundays and stood at the back of the church for a little while.

"You haven't been serving mass."

"No," I said. "No, I'm concentrating on basketball."

"You should tell them you're quitting then," said Helen.

"All right."

"Gil served till last year," she said to me.

"Gil didn't play anything," I said.

We sipped our Pepsi for a little bit. Helen was rigid but extremely smart. I'd much rather talk to Sam about this kind of stuff because then I knew what we were talking about was really what we were talking about.

"Have you been meeting girls?" she said.

"Sally?" I said.

"Secretly?" said Helen. "I want you to promise me you won't sneak off with girls."

I had to make that promise. I had to lie. If it was just about church and girls, then Helen didn't know the half of it. But that Christmas I got an indication that someone else in the family did. My older sister, Aubrey, bought me a flask. "For my alcoholic little brother," she said. I had just turned fourteen. Everybody laughed.

But before that, in the fall, Callahan began getting me ready for high school. We began our daily workouts again, followed by physical therapy. On the couch in his small TV room Callahan brought me to climax, which by then was something I really desired, because the tension of going ten, fifteen, twenty minutes under the hand job, time and again being brought to the verge of coming and then pulled away, had become maddening. After everything else, the pain and the intimacy, ejaculation seemed an irrelevant step. Callahan acted surprised the first time I came, even a little disgusted. He stood, then threw me a towel and told me to clean up. But never again would I have physical therapy without an orgasm.

He wanted to know about Tommy Cale. After therapy, he pulled me down by the hair until my head rested in the crook of his elbow, or he turned me to him and we talked face to face, our chests almost touching. If I resisted in any way he forced me to grapple with him, though he was quick to grab my hair or balls if I achieved an advantage. He called it masculine, like the Greeks.

"I've heard Tommy Cale is a bit effeminate," Callahan said to me.

"No," I said.

"He wears his hair long and he doesn't play any sports."

"He plays guitar," I said.

"What do you have in common?" said Callahan.

"He's going out with Sally's best friend," I said. "And we listen to music."

"Well, there's nothing wrong with a friendship based on utility," said Callahan.

"Aristotle classified friendships of utility as the lowest and most common. Probably the best word for that kind of casual friend," he said, "is *acquaintance*. Like Kenny Bruce. You want him to be your friend, but he doesn't have the stuff for real friendship. He's amiable, but weak-natured and unreliable. You need someone strong, who you can't run roughshod over, someone who will always be there."

"I just want somebody to hang out with," I said. "Not marry."

He pulled me down by the hair. A lecture was coming. "Let's keep it respectful, Mr. Rosenthal," he said. "If you're lucky, someday you'll find a woman who'll give you love and friendship, but I doubt it. In general women don't understand men. Even those who do, who understand the necessity of giving themselves over to a man, they have needs like clothes and children. Women are monogamous by nature," he said. "That suits the demands of maintaining a family. Women are possessive and passive. They seek security in the life of the home, while the instincts of men are active, out-going and polygamous."

I was unlikely to find another young man to meet the intense demands of my friendship, said Callahan. Only a special kind of man could meet me on the plane of Aristotle's highest form of friendship, a friendship he called *Platonic*, which involved the love of a man for a boy, the love of a mentor, erudite and wise, for an exceptional boy ready to learn. For the first time he mentioned Hadrian and Antinous, and how the Roman troops cheered when the stoic, lonely Hadrian took the lovely slave boy into his tent. He spoke of Achilles and Patroclus, of Alexander the Great and how he wept and raged for a week after the death of his best friend. He gave me Gore Vidal's *Julian* and Mary Renault's *The Persian Boy*.

Callahan asked me to think about the Greek statues I'd seen in the Cleveland Museum. All I could remember was how the sexual organs seemed so small. Forget that, he said. For years the penis and testicles were covered by grape leaves, a vestige of the absurd moral power of the Catholic Church. No, think of the forms of those statues. The beauty and symmetry of the male body, graceful, muscular, unlike the imperfect female form with its soft, bulbous flaws. Sure, said Callahan, we desire those female bodies. We desire them. But think of it aesthetically. Who in their right mind could see the female body as more beautiful than the male?

He got up and came back to the couch with a picture of Michelangelo's *David*. There was the perfect form. How did mine compare? He told me then that the model for *David* was not a boy who lived in Michelangelo's time. The form of *David* was copied from the thousands of sculptures the mourning Hadrian had made of his boy, Antinous, after Antinous' death. Antinous, he said, so feared aging that he committed suicide in his early twenties, rather than grow old and unattractive to Hadrian.

Released by his attention to the book, I got up to dress.

"So you're still with Sally?" he said.

"Yes," I said. "Of course.

"A passing fancy," said Callahan. "You're both children."

"That's why it's a good thing," I said unconsciously.

"It's not a good thing," he said.

He stood there in the dark, his T-shirt tucked into his jockey shorts, his dark socks pulled to his knees. His belly bulged. White, dry scales from psoriasis flaked on his naked thighs. This was the god who had descended to make me a man. It seemed, almost, in that moment, that he was aware of a nascent scrutiny I was yet unable to articulate.

"Have a girlfriend, by all means," said Callahan. "You'll have plenty of women someday." But on the drive home he reminded me that I had things to accomplish. Girls took time. Boys who were pursuing girls or going steady would make nothing of their lives. "In a few years they'll be married with kids and crummy jobs. Nothings," he said. Undisciplined dreamers who would wake up at forty and look back on their wasted lives and then, maybe, rise to the highest moment of their humanity by wondering what might have been.

Besides, right then, time I took away from basketball could mean the end of my fragile hopes of making the team at St. Mike's Prep.

But I didn't even want to go to St. Mike's. How could I, if I took my atheism seriously? Now I resented my mother's Catholicism, my father's brutish simplicity, my family's poverty. Now the money I'd saved by working my paper routes would be used to pay my tuition. But Callahan convinced me that I wasn't ready to compete against inner-city talent, black kids, who flooded the public junior highs.

That autumn Dan Callahan moved to a new townhouse in a development just south of the German ghetto where my father was raised. I told Callahan that Helen was looking to go back to work, and now a Dean at St. Mary's College, he offered her a job as the college receptionist. He told my parents that he'd help Aubrey get a scholarship.

And I began the semester at St. Mike's Prep. Seniors beat me up for my lunch money, or sometimes just beat me up. The teachers were stern and unreasonable, particularly the secular ones, athletic coaches who really didn't want to be in the classroom. They controlled their classes through intimidation, physical beatings, and public humiliation. In swim class we stripped, showered, and swam nude. The teacher lined us up in front of him and walked up and down the line of naked boys, whipping us across our upper thighs with his lanyard.

By now, Callahan was already a powerful man in town. Though St. Mike's had only a J.V. team at the time, Callahan convinced the powers there to re-institute their freshman basketball program to compete with the public junior high schools. Once a local basketball power, St. Mike's hadn't had a winning varsity basketball season in years and Callahan convinced them that a freshman team, added to the J.V. team, would double their chances of developing young talent. He finagled the freshman coaching job for a young friend of his, Freddy Dale.

For my part, unable to teach me a straight up jump shot and with my ball handling skills too weak for me to play guard, Callahan prepared me to try out as a small forward. I was a little over five-nine. Along with my rolling hooks, which I shot both right and left handed, he used my tendency to lean off my back foot to teach me a fade-away jump shot. Falling away, I learned to bring the ball above my head and straighten out a tendency I had to drop my right shoulder as I shot. Callahan improved my foul shooting from 50% to 80% by having me line up with my right toe on the foul line just off-center to the right of the hoop, and my right shoulder turned to the basket. For both the fade-away jumper and the foul shot, he spent hours watching me and adjusting my release until we found something that worked.

"Yes!" Callahan yelled as I began to hit the fade-away. "Yes! We'll make a basketball player out of you yet!"

By try-out time in November I could hit the fade-away regularly over a taller man. And as a favor to Callahan for getting him the job, Freddy Dale kept three Holy Name players on his freshman team: Wooj as a starting forward, Kenny Bruce at back-up guard, and me as fifteenth man on a fifteen man squad.

I found that I wasn't that good. My defense was poor, my ball handling inept. Working inside, I was completely dependent on somebody getting me the ball unless I rebounded over taller men. I blamed my problems on abandoning my old shoulder shot for the new fade-away. Callahan assured me that I was thinking short term. I'd never get anywhere with the old shot. Building on the fade-away jumper, I'd done the impossible. I'd found an available niche. In a year I'd gone from thirteenth man at Holy Name to making the freshman team at St. Mike's. I'd beaten out hundreds of kids who only a year ago were far better than me.

Tommy Cale soon confirmed Callahan's predictions by telling me that he really wasn't interested in Diane anymore. He said he really wasn't interested in girls at all. He'd kept his relationship with Diane through the summer so he could hang out with me. He was joining a rock band. When he told me, I punched him. He looked at me, dazed, and I hit him again. Glasses tilted on his head, he turned from me and walked away.

Within the week I dumped Sally Thomas, too. After getting off the city bus that we caught together so I could walk her home from school, I told her that I didn't want to walk her home, that I didn't want to see her anymore. She stood in front of me and cried. Only a few weeks ago she'd been my first love and now, suddenly, when I looked at her I felt only aversion. But if I loathed her in person, then at night, in Callahan's arms, I imagined myself behind her blue eyes, her hair as my hair, falling across my naked shoulders, my tiny nipples as her full breasts, my lips as hers, pressing against Callahan's.

One afternoon Callahan took my old, winter coat that had been handed down to me from a neighbor and threw it in the gutter. He bought me a new one, safari style, woolen, with a belt. He took me out for *filet mignon*, bought me shoes and sweaters, took me to the movies, shared cocktails with me. He was powerful, educated, wise. My life depended on him. I loved him. He was God.

That fall my therapy took its final turn. Once Callahan got me hard, he took Vaseline and coated my penis, then turned me to him and had me shove me my penis between his thighs. Covering my mouth with his, he had me plunge my penis in and out between his legs. This thrusting, he said, was excellent for loosening and tightening my groin. Covering my mouth, he said, created heat. He wore Jockey shorts. I was naked as he held my ass, gripped my hair, and pushed me into him until I came.

In a few weeks he moved the therapy from his couch to his bed and afterward, always, he wanted to wrestle and talk. When we wrestled, I fought back and he pulled my hair and used his unshaven beard as a weapon on my face and skin. I hated the thick, greasy Vaseline that caked my organs and spread to my thighs, groin, and chest.

I always wanted to get up immediately and wash it all away, but Callahan pinned me beneath him, his hands in my hair. His hands stroking me, I learned the history of Rome, the battles of Hannibal and Caesar, the imperial rule of Augustus, Tiberius, Caligula, Claudius, and Nero. I read biographies of Charlemagne and Constantine the Great. I read Robert Graves' *I, Claudius* and *Claudius the God*. On to the American Revolution and the founding of the greatest nation on earth. And though I barely noticed his penis during sex, afterward I saw the yellow stain of cum on his Jockey's and felt the cold, sticky remnants of his semen on my skin.

Chapter Sixteen

I went to him. I went to him again and again. I went to him because I wanted to become a basketball star. I went because I wanted to be his favorite. Because I wanted to get drunk. Because I was afraid of girls. Because sometimes I wanted to run from everything: from my parents and family, from the oppression of my teachers, even from the things that Callahan wanted me to become—a great man, a great basketball player.

The hours I once spent playing sports games in my mind, or talking to God, were now filled with fantasies about waking up changed into my latest infatuation, helpless in the body of a girl. Then I didn't have to grow up to be a great man. I didn't have to hold a job or be an athlete. I could spend my days the way I did with Tommy Cale, listening to records and talking about clothes.

Still small enough to fit in Helen's and Aubrey's clothes, I stayed home sick from school and tried on their underwear and bras, girdles and nylons, dresses, skirts, scarves and shoes. Confining and uncomfortable, they didn't excite me so much as the fantasy of owning the body and life that had to wear them, idealizing the life of a girl and reducing it to trying on clothes and having breasts, transforming passivity into the power of choosing which boy I'd date, though I never picked out a specific boy in my daydreams, or even kissed one. I had the night for that, when I endured Callahan's manhandling with passive, ambivalent female lust.

That freshman fall, Callahan arranged a double-date for me and Wooj. I went out with Mara Kent, once the star of Holy Name's girls' basketball team, and Wooj with Huffy Robert's little sister, Darlene. Wooj's father drove us to the freshman mixer at St. Mike's gym. Both ex-tomboys, now these desperate girls had piled up and sprayed their hair like a pair of fifty-year-olds and put on false eyelashes and too much make-up. Attempting to avoid romance at all costs, I behaved like a maniac. At the end of the night I shook Mara's hand. In four years of high school, I never dated again.

I lived and breathed basketball and Callahan. After school I did my homework at the Woolworth's soda fountain while waiting for the Varsity and then the J.V.s to finish practice. After basketball practice I took the bus home, ate the food my mom had saved for me from dinner, then called Callahan for another workout. When my sinuses ached, he cleared them. When I pulled muscles, Callahan put them back in. Sometimes when I showed up at his townhouse I had to wait in line behind high school jocks, grade school wannabes, even parents who came to him for the cure. Often he invited people in to see what he was doing, showing what muscle was out, how the matrix of muscles was layered, how he'd put it back. He explained physiology, advised preventative measures, handed out aspirin and Ace Bandages.

Though I applied myself in the classroom, besides algebra and earth science, in which I had little interest, there seemed little that school could offer me. If we read *A Separate Peace* in English, well, I'd already read it, along with *Catcher in the Rye*, *The Lord of the Flies*, *Great Expectations*, and *The Great Gatsby*. If we read *Brave New World* in class, then I'd already read *The Communist Manifesto*, *The Tempest*, *Animal Farm*, and *1984*. I grew cynical and Callahan fed it.

"Teachers, like most human beings, are lazy and mediocre," he said.

We sat at his kitchen table. I cooked for him now when I was there, that night broiling two, huge porterhouse steaks and baking frozen Tater Tots. He drank scotch and water. I drank beer.

"You must rise above it," he said. "It is the battle all great men fight."

"They don't see it," I said. "They don't see their mediocrity and they don't recognize greatness."

"But some men rise above them anyway. Arthur. Churchill. Kennedy."

"No one sees themselves for what they are," I said to him. "There's no mirror for intelligence, bravery, inner beauty."

"Inner beauty. Ha! Mr. Rosenthal. You are something. Now finish that steak and get upstairs."

Upstairs is where it always ended up, and more and more I realized that it was something he couldn't see, even if he looked in the mirror.

On the basketball floor, I struggled and my team struggled more. In the first half of our season we won one game. Freddy Dale, thin and wiry with short, thick, black hair, tried to motivate us, his team of white kids, by telling us we shouldn't let ourselves be manhandled by a bunch of niggers. God might have given them more talent, but we had intelligence and discipline. Before games he'd finish his pep talk with, "Now go out there and kick ass on those niggers!" Then those undisciplined niggers kicked our asses. I finally went up to him after a practice and said, "Coach, my neighborhood is mostly black. Some of those niggers are my neighbors."

"I didn't mean it that way," said Freddy Dale. "I'm sorry." And he stopped using the word.

Callahan laughed hard when I told him. "Some of those niggers are my neighbors! Mr. Rosenthal, you do have a way with words. And a naiveté that pierces the soul."

My naiveté aside, by mid-season a desperate Freddy Dale tried me in a few games. Facing bigger kids who were stronger than me, I was scared as hell, good only for a few points and a couple rebounds. Though the Wooj still started, Kenny Bruce was long gone. I started once, played horribly, and was benched. Now even Callahan admitted that I couldn't play forward and that very night we worked until two a.m. in St. Mary's College dark basement gym to teach me a jump shot. It felt glorious as I leapt into the air, released, and nailed shot after shot. But he didn't stop there. Working off months of previous practice, he taught me the rocker step, a way of leaping into a dribble-drive to the basket. He pushed my left-hand dribbling so hard that by the beginning of our second half league schedule I moved better to the left than the right. Suddenly, from twenty feet out, I could go left or right and be at the basket in one dribble, or pull up for the jumper.

Callahan came to our freshman practice and had me demonstrate my rocker step and jump shot to Freddy Dale who started me the next game at weak-side guard. I scored fourteen points and we won. With me starting at guard, we finished the year .500. Callahan had worked another miracle.

Chapter Seventeen

One afternoon that next summer I took a walk with Wooj's little brother, the Little Wooj. I used to like to walk up to Carney Street, where Wooj and Kenny lived. My neighborhood had grown tough. Home owners moved and began renting houses to poor families. As landlords, they didn't keep up the property. Things got run down; there were drugs for sale, a whorehouse down the street, a corner bar with fights and guns. Out Carney Street there were wide, one-story houses with green lawns. We played basketball in Kenny's driveway, Wooj and Kenny against me and Little Wooj.

Little Wooj and I now beat them pretty regularly. We played hard, fought bitterly, then I'd end up with Little Wooj, taking walks in the woody hills above St. Mary's. Little Wooj was always kind of a free-wheeling kid, and on one of those walks he said to me, "What do you think of old Callahan? Kind of a weirdo, huh?"

"What do you mean?" I said.

"What do I mean," smirked Little Wooj, rolling his eyes. "Queer." Little Wooj followed me at Holy Name by two years, in fact I'd coached him in sixth grade intramurals. After Huffy and Herbie's team lost in the city title game, it was Little Wooj's team that started a run of city titles that covered two decades. Little Wooj, Donnie was his name, was lighter skinned, lighter haired, and less brooding than Big Wooj.

"Who said that?" I said. "Your brother?"

"My brother doesn't have a clue," said Donnie Wooj. "Huffy does, though."

"What did Huffy say?"

"Called him a little weird," Little Wooj said.

"Callahan demands a lot of loyalty," I said.

"You bet," said Donnie. "That's the word I was looking for. Loyalty."

A number of kids, like Raymond Luciani, and Kenny Bruce now, too, actually hid from Callahan. Once, driving down the street, Callahan and I spotted Kenny Bruce hiding behind a bush. "What the hell?" said Callahan. "That crazy kid. What's he doing?"

"Hiding from you," I said.

"Why would anyone hide from me?" said the astonished Callahan.

"Because he's afraid," I said.

"Afraid? Afraid of what?"

"You," I said again. "Your power." I couldn't express it, but somehow each of us felt as if we were the only one. We couldn't speak to each other. We felt ashamed. I understood that shame without understanding anything else at all. I became female. Kenny hid.

"My power?" said Callahan. "My power?"

"He failed you," I said. "He's afraid of you."

"That's nuts," said Callahan. He never saw himself as part of the problem. Yet the choice to "not make anything of yourself," allowed you to be "written off"—another Callahan phrase—and once and finally "written off to become a nothing," you were free, at least free of Callahan, even if you couldn't face him.

I'd said nothing to Little Wooj for a while. We sat down under an apple tree. Donnie picked up and tasted the little apples from the ground, took one bite and threw them away.

"How does Huffy know?" I said.

"About Callahan?" said Little Wooj.

"Has Callahan done anything to him?"

"To Huffy? I doubt it."

"Then how would he know?"

"That's a good one on Huffy," Donnie said.

"What does the Big Wooj say about it?" I asked Donnie.

"He's so thick, I don't think he's got a clue what's going on," Donnie Wooj said.

"What about you?" I said.

"Come on," he said. "You're the favorite. You're no dummy. A little nooky for free beer. It's okay."

But Big Wooj did have a clue. Once that same summer, walking home together from the Y, the Wooj asked me, "Has Callahan ever done anything weird to you?"

"What do you mean?"

"You know," said the Wooj, looking away. "You know, in bed."

"It's a little weird sometimes," I said.

"Yeah," said Wooj, "a little weird." And we never spoke of it again.

I felt a little weird. I was now fourteen. Lying chest to chest with Callahan, his hands in my hair and his mouth on mine, plunging my penis between his rough, liquid thighs; it felt like sex to me. But who would you talk to? Who would you tell? And the risk of mentioning it to Callahan himself was that I could lose everything.

That summer, before visiting again with Callahan at Ohio State, I read history: Herodotus and Thucydides, Plutarch, Cicero, histories of Greece, Rome, the American Revolution, the Civil War. He assigned me a paper to be completed by the time I met him in Columbus. I studied the battles of Caesar, Alexander the Great, Hannibal, and Napoleon, analyzed them, then argued that Hannibal was the best general.

"Why Hannibal?" said Callahan, holding the forty page tome in front of him.

"He crossed the Alps and spent fifteen years in Italy," I said. "The others were good strategists and used systems like the phalanx or the legion. Hannibal was fluid. He used his opponents' strengths against them."

"I'll read this closely, Mr. Rosenthal," Callahan said.

Later that visit, Freddy Dale came through town. We visited some underground caves in West Virginia, drove over to the Pro Football Hall of Fame in Canton. Though Dale praised my hard work and improvement, the trip was tense and awkward, and I felt as if he wanted something from me, something, praise, appreciation. Of course, I was only a boy. I couldn't understand his ambitions. But they came out that night, back in Columbus, at a pizza bar. Dale was on his second beer and Callahan on his third rum and coke when the pizza came. I'd gotten to the point where eating in public was a pain in the ass, because I couldn't get drunk.

"I'll never get past Olsen," he said, "even if Murphy leaves." Murphy was the varsity coach and under a lot of pressure after three losing seasons. Roger Olsen was the notorious head coach of J.V. football and basketball who won titles by toughness and attrition. No one could understand why his winning J.V. teams faltered on the varsity level, but in fact most of the other high schools pulled their best sophomores to play varsity.

"Murphy will be fired after this year," said Callahan. "He has nothing. It'll be his last disaster. You'll move up to J.V."

"Olsen will take over," Freddy Dale moaned, "and he doesn't like me."

Callahan glanced at me, then looked back at Dale. He finally pushed his rum and coke across the table to me and I took a long hit.

"Careful," said Freddy.

"Olsen isn't the whole game. I'll help you," said Callahan.

"You?" said Freddy Dale.

"I'll do what I can," Callahan said. "Olsen has his friends. I have friends, too."

"I'll be squeezed out by the old boys and Olsen, those violent bastards," moaned Dale. He ordered a third beer and Callahan ordered rum and coke again.

"I hate them, too," I said. I sipped from Callahan's drink again.

Dale leapt at me. "Those are your teachers and coaches," he said. "Respect them."

"You were just bitching about them," Callahan said to him. "You expect the boy not to follow your lead?"

Dale recoiled, hurt, but before he replied the bartender was standing over our table.

"What the hell are you doing?" he said to Callahan.

"We're having a conversation," Callahan said.

"You're giving that kid your drink," the man said. He was big bellied and wore a stained apron.

"I was not," Callahan said.

The bartender threw his rag on the table. "You were. I saw you."

"I can do what I want with my drink," Callahan insisted.

"Not in my bar. How old is that kid? He's a child. What kind of man are you?"

Now Callahan pounded the table. "Are you accusing me?"

"I know what I saw. Why would you get a kid drunk? I'm taking your drinks away."

"You can have the drinks and the pizza, too," said Callahan. "We're leaving."

"I'm throwing you out," the bartender said. He began to yell. "I want you out! Now!"

Dale had already hustled away from the table and I'd followed. As Callahan got up, the big bartender pushed him in the chest with the heel of his hand. People were watching now. "Out you pervert, now! I'm calling the cops!"

"Call them," said Callahan. "Call them." But he backed away and met us at the door for our exit. As we walked back to the dorms Callahan fumed, but Dale and I walked beside him in silence. I'd heard this indignation before, the night in his apartment when he first asked me to take off my clothes. Once, Freddy murmured, "You can't give the kid drinks in public."

"What," said Callahan, "a sip of coke and rum. It's idiotic."

For my part, I knew he was right. The rules were simple-minded and stupid. Not for one of the apostles. Not for me. The bartender had things at stake. In a society of simple rules, he was a simple man with simple things to protect. Even Freddy Dale didn't get it, even if now he resented it. I only wished that the bartender didn't remind me of Sam.

That fall, I handed my summer research paper to my history teacher on the first day of class. The old priest raised an eyebrow. "What's this?"

"This summer," I said. "I researched it on my own."

That kind of intellectual virtue couldn't go unpunished. The old priest ignored the paper and it wasn't long before I was perceived as a disruption in the classroom. Word spread. Soon my precociousness was seen as defiance. Soon after that, it was.

In Theology I argued against creationism and for atheism and evolution. In social science I wrote a paper against America's use of the atomic bomb on Hiroshima and Nagasaki. I blamed the United States for consequent nuclear proliferation as well as political duplicity and came down hard on the American refusal to reject first-strike nuclear policy.

Now even Callahan was getting edgy with me. He read the paper and told me that he respected my right to dissent, but he thought I made a big mistake in judgment. The American first-strike threat created a balance of power, he argued, which prevented the Russians and Chinese from acting rashly. In World War Two the bomb saved thousands of American lives, including the life of my father who was in the Pacific at the time.

"Ask your father what he thinks," said Callahan, and I did.

Sam said, "I was a Marine. I would have killed anybody they told me to. The bomb ended the war. I hated the Japanese. I was happy."

"But what do you think about it now?" I asked him.

"You think they wouldn't have bombed us?" my dad said. "It's over. There's nothing to think about it now. Now everybody's driving Japanese and German cars."

Sam's Razor. My father read the machinations of the world as simple and personal.

But my mother said the bomb was wrong. "When it happened I was happy," she said. "But then I saw the pictures. If we hadn't dropped the bomb, maybe your father would have been killed and you wouldn't exist, but if there's a nuclear war, which I worry about every day, then you'll be dead anyways." She looked at me in that deep, sorrowful way she had, full of longing and fear and love. "So say the rosary every day," she said.

I went back to Callahan and told him my position was unchanged.

"Don't be crazy," he said. "Learn to keep those kinds of thoughts to yourself."

But I couldn't. During my freshman year, Callahan had ghost written a letter from me to the editor of the *Stuben Times*, denouncing the Vietnicks. It was published and I got some notoriety. Now, in my sophomore year, I wrote a paper for my History class reversing my position, saying our stand in Vietnam was anachronistic Cold War diplomacy, that the Domino Theory, and the theory of territorial footholds, were myths. I said we were fighting a war for French imperialism. We should get out.

My history teacher said nothing. Without comment, I got the paper back with a *C*. But the next day in first period English my instructor, an assistant football coach, asked me to follow him into the hall. There he put his hand on my throat and jacked me up against the lockers. He banged me against them, wham, wham, again and again. He grabbed my tie and pulled it up, hanging me there under his fist. "We've fucking had it with you," he said. "Shut up. Just shut the fuck up. No more papers. No more opinions. Nothing." In every class I was placed behind the last row of desks

at the back of the room. The rule was, shut up and take a *C.*
But if it had only been that simple. My English instructor regularly pulled me out of the classroom to rough me up and tear my
red blazer, part of our school uniform. Next period I'd be given
demerits for torn clothes and thrown out of class, only to receive
more demerits for being in the hallway without a pass. Teachers
held me out of class until after the bell, then sent me to the office
for being late. If I was absent, my mother's notes were torn up and
I was declared delinquent. In no time at all I received permanent
detention and had to attend school on Saturday mornings. Helen
threatened to make an appointment with the vice-principal, but I
begged her to stay out of it. She'd only make things worse.

"Why?" said Sam. "What are you doing wrong?"

"It's because I'm smart," I said.

"Then wise up and don't be so smart," said Sam.

My only reprieve came during detention itself, where the moni-
tor, an effeminate administrator named Fr. Dee took me aside one
afternoon.

"Feeling like Job?" he said.

"A little."

He had sandy, blond hair that he combed back in a wave, gentle
blue eyes, immaculate hands and soft, white skin. "A boy like you,"
he said. He put his hands over his mouth and looked at me. "There's
a price for being different," he said. "And maybe so good-looking."

I said nothing as he watched me. Dee was considerate and gentle
in an atmosphere that was often sadistic and homophobic. Gentle
priests, as well as gentle boys, were constantly earmarked as queers
by the jocks and Dee was no exception. But I wasn't afraid of any
of that. What might he do, touch me?

"Well," he said, "you're already on permanent detention. What
else can they do? They won't expel you. Soon, they might need you.
But Mr. Rosenthal," said Fr. Dee, "let's learn to keep our opinions,
our inner beliefs, on the inside. It's all right to have secrets. Really."

After that, without saying more, when I showed up for detention on Saturday mornings, Dee sent me to the rectory where I
washed floors or windows, though after a while I just went to Fr.
Dee's room and read. After he let out detention, Dee came by and
we ate lunch in the kitchen of the rectory. One afternoon, after
lunch, he told me not to show up for detention anymore. He'd just

mark me present. Keep my mouth shut about it and stay away, unless I wanted to drop by and talk with him.

Callahan said he had no sympathy for me. I was too honest. I got what I deserved. Besides, my positions portrayed my cowardice, ignorance, and sophomoric reasoning. Worst of all, I was unpatriotic. I was being disloyal to my country.

I stood in front of him. "Patriotism is an evil which creates war," I said.

"Get out of here!" yelled Dan Callahan. "I will not have those ideas in my house!"

"Okay," I said. "If that's the way you feel, okay."

But as I gathered to go, he stopped me. "Let's talk about it some other time," said Dan Callahan. "Now get upstairs."

I now understood that as long as I submitted to therapy, I could think and say almost anything I pleased.

But my war was expanding on several other fronts. Aubrey, now a high school senior, pulled me aside.

"What's up with you and Callahan?" she said.

"What do you mean, 'what's up?' Nothing's up."

"You see too much of him. It's too strange."

"I play basketball," I said. "He teaches me basketball."

"He takes you out to dinner. You go to movies. He buys you clothes."

"You're jealous," I said.

"Yes, a little. I'm not the only one in the house who's jealous. But I don't want what you have." Aubrey was fair skinned with dark, auburn hair, and though overweight as a child, now she was thin and striking, and extremely bright.

"You tell me then," I said. "If you know so much, tell me."

"I know enough," she said, "to know something's wrong when I see it. Something's wrong and I'm telling Mom."

"What are you going to tell her? What's to know?"

"It will be based on what she already knows, dear little brother. Based on it."

But my parents were good hearted people, busy people. My father landed a new job selling construction material and worked long hours. My mother worked full time as a receptionist, then came home and tried to manage, cook and clean house for eight. Gil was struggling in college and he and Sam fought over grades.

Now Aubrey was going to Helen about Callahan. But what could she know?

Nothing happened till my first quarter grades came in the mail, all *C*'s. My parents pulled me aside.

"The *C*'s are just punishment for my ideas," I said. "They don't even let me talk in class, write papers or take tests anymore."

"Maybe it's because of Callahan," my mother said. "I'm not so sure he's good for you."

"Callahan disagrees with my ideas, too."

"Not about God," said Helen. "He's ruined your faith."

"He goes to church," I said. "You see him in church."

"At the back," she said. "He doesn't take communion. And neither do you."

"I don't want you to see him after supper anymore," said Sam. "Not until you get your grades back up."

"I can't get my grades back up!" I screamed.

Sam got up and stepped into me, grabbing my shirt. "Not at your mother," he said. "Never raise your voice to your mother."

I said, "I'm sorry." After a little bit I said, "Callahan has done good for everyone. Look at all the coaches and lawyers, teachers, doctors, even congressmen."

"Not after supper," said Sam. "That's final."

I was almost relieved to tell Callahan.

"Why that's absurd," he said.

In a month, Helen was promoted to Administrative Assistant to the Dean of St. Mary's College, Dan Callahan. She got a raise. Sam got a big contract to refurbish Holy Name's basketball floor and reconstruct the gym. Aubrey received a full academic scholarship to St. Mary's. Basketball season started. And I was seeing Callahan after supper again. Neither of my parents ever knew about me and Dan. How could they know the unimaginable? They never did.

Chapter Eighteen

The year softened into basketball season. During the summer, head varsity coach, Tom Murphy, had held summer workouts. I played well; in fact Murphy told me he couldn't tell if I was right or left handed. He asked me if I wanted to skip J.V. and play varsity, but as soon as Callahan caught wind of it he cut it off at the pass. He convinced Murphy I needed game experience that I wouldn't get on the varsity bench.

I was disappointed. "I want to play varsity," I told him. I wanted the prestige. City League varsity games were played in the Stuben Civic Auditorium, in front of up to five thousand fans. And the varsity was weak. By the end of the season Murphy would have to dump his seniors and think of next year. I might play. I resented Callahan's interference.

"Play J.V." he said. "Be a star."

And I wanted to avoid the J.V. coach, too. Roger Olsen had a brutal temper. He didn't even cut the team during try-outs. He ran us and ranted at us until kids just withered away. Kenny Bruce lasted a week. Once Olsen began practice by saying that we were going to shoot lay-ups until somebody missed, even if we shot lay-ups all night.

"I bet it's going to be Larry Womack," he said. "And when you miss, Larry, I'm going to punch out your lights. I bet you miss the first time, Womack," said Olsen. "If you make the first one, I'll give the team a day off and if you miss I'm going to punch your lights out."

Womack choked on his first lay-up. Olsen ran after him, chasing him until he caught him against the bleachers, then pounding him with body punches. In tears, Larry Womack left the gym and never came back.

A short, powerful man, Olsen scared the life out of me. But I wasn't his whipping boy. It was the Wooj. Unable to hold two things in his mind at one time, all he could hold was his fear. When Wooj wasn't frozen in fright, he ran around the gym like a headless chicken, launching shots from anywhere he got the ball. It sent Olsen into a rage. Wooj panicked more. Once, Olsen took off after him, chasing the Wooj around the gym like something out of the Keystone Cops. Finally, Wooj ran out of the gym. Olsen followed, still raging, chasing Wooj outside where Olsen locked him out in the snow. "Counting the days till the end of the season, Wojesewski?" bellowed Olsen. "Well I'm counting them too! Quit!" Olsen yelled. "Come on, please quit!" But the Wooj never quit. He didn't play a minute that season, but he never quit.

Olsen called me Dudley Doo-Right because I meticulously followed his instructions. Then I lit up the scoreboard in our league opener. After that he took to calling me Chuckie. He yelled from the sidelines during tight games, "Pass the ball to Chuckie! Give the fucking ball to Chuckie!" After practices he took me to the Y to use the stream bath for my sinuses. And once we began winning, Roger Olsen calmed down.

After dropping our first two games, we won twenty out of twenty-one and won the city championship, going undefeated in league play. I led the league in scoring. The one game we lost was to the team who beat us in our opener, a mediocre bunch from a tiny, county school. The second time, after they'd upset us on our home floor, Olsen just shrugged. He put his arm over my shoulder. "Some teams just have your number, don't you think?" he said.

After the season Olsen had a serious auto accident and came out of the hospital a changed man, gentle and thoughtful, careful to check his temper. Callahan convinced him to quit coaching, helped him get into graduate school and then hired him to teach at St. Mary's while completing his degree.

"I thought you hated him for what he did to Wooj," I said to Callahan.

"That's irrelevant," said Callahan. "Now he'll never ruin another one of my kids."

That spring, after my success on J.V., the academic situation at St. Mike's softened for me, too. My chemistry teacher, the swim coach, moved me back into the class seating and said, "Just do the work and everything will be okay." Soon, the other coaches did the same, and when the assistant football coach approached me about playing halfback or flanker in the fall, I wisely said I'd consider it.

The success of my J.V. season made both my parents proud. That summer, at the cost of $700, Sam buckled to my request that we build a basketball court in our backyard. He and I dug out the lawn ourselves, pounded the ground flat and squared up the wooden frame for the concrete pour. We built the basket ourselves, too: the stand out of pipes welded by a friend of Sam's, the backboard from plywood and laminated board, then a cement truck rolled in and poured the concrete. Sam and I helped flatten the cement with long boards, then I watered it for a week so it would dry slow and solid. While the court dried, I helped Sam put up a ten foot wire fence around the side of the yard, digging and cementing in the long, steel poles, then stretching the metal fence with a fence stretcher. Finally, the evening that Sam painted a blue basketball key in front of the basket on the dry cement, Aubrey walked onto the court and smeared the new paint with her shoes.

"Fuck you!" she yelled at Sam. She pointed at me. "Fuck you!" And finally, at Helen, "Fuck you!"

That was the one *fuck you* over the line for Sam, who followed her into the house and up the stairs to the girls' room. We heard her out the window. "We're poor! We're fucking poor!" she yelled. "I can't get a new goddamn pair of shoes!"

It was quiet then before Aubrey ran down the stairs again and into the yard. "What's it going to take?" yelled Aubrey. "Fuck all of you!"

My parents stood quietly in front of her, my younger brothers, Joseph and Andy there, Sylvie, and the neighbors. Aubrey walked up to Helen. She put a finger in her face. "Fuck you," she said. "Fuck you. Fuck you. Fuck you."

Sam took her by the hair and dragged her inside. And he hit her. We could hear her yelp.

After that Aubrey fought with my parents constantly, though to my mind Aubrey had always fought with them bitterly and constantly about everything and the basketball court was just something more bitter and more constant. Sometimes she locked herself into her and Sylvie's room. Sometimes she ran through the house screaming and throwing things. Other times she yelled, spitting in Sam's face, "Fuck! Fuck! Fuck!" until he threatened her and she yelled "Fuck you!" again. If he didn't respond then, she'd find Helen and begin yelling "Fuck you!" until Sam finally slapped her until she shut up.

It was working class life. Other families had kids in prison or on the streets. Aubrey was a brilliant daughter, a good artist, a voluminous reader, an excellent essayist; probably the brightest person in our family, and a bit high strung. She hated Callahan and she hated me for the things he gave me. In the battle for my parents' limited resources, no amount of new Easter outfits added up to that basketball court in money or emphasis. Nothing could take the place of the time my parents spent watching me play basketball. She had nothing to match the clothes and shoes that Callahan bought for me.

I brought up Aubrey's tantrums to Callahan. He said, "What Aubrey doesn't understand is how hard you work for what you get from me, what you've given up, what you have to do every day." That was what Aubrey didn't understand.

When Roger Olsen resigned as St. Mike's J.V. coach, Callahan got Freddy Dale the job. Though something had changed between Callahan and Dale. Callahan used his influence to topple Tom Murphy, who'd gone 3–21 that winter, and got the head coaching job at St. Mike's for a friend of his from a small school in Connenville, Ohio, Larry LaRuche. To facilitate it, Callahan volunteered to coach St. Mike's freshman team for free until they could find a replacement.

Dale struggled in his first year with the J.V.s because LaRuche, like other varsity coaches, now lifted the best sophomores. Callahan won the grade school state title, going 33–1, and won the freshman league title, too, at 27–0. While Callahan pressed LaRuche to play an up-tempo style game, Dale, now Larry LaRuche's assistant, stressed ball handling and defense. Insecure in his first year as coach, LaRuche played only his seniors. He argued to Callahan that they were more cohesive as a group and that the seniors didn't like me. Though as a substitute I averaged more than a point a minute, Freddy Dale said I was a poor ball handler, a bad defensive player, and a selfish shooter. As the season progressed and the seniors won, with Dale next to La Ruche on the bench, I played less and less.

Enraged, I played more basketball than ever, working out at Holy Name and then back at St. Mike's with Callahan's freshman team after every varsity practice, and then yet again, at night, individually with Callahan. And though Callahan campaigned constantly to LaRuche on my behalf, it seemed to work against me. My constant association with Callahan and his teams gave the impression that I was more loyal to him than to St. Mike's. And though Callahan couldn't see it, LaRuche, as well as Dale, feared Callahan's success and ambition.

"I'm a college professor and a Dean," Callahan said to me when I brought it up. "What do I care about the power politics of high school athletics? I want to help boys learn by winning."

Caught between Dale's antipathy and LaRuche's apprehension, I saw Callahan more and more as my only ally, and feared his power to abandon me. I drank a lot. At night. On road trips. At Callahan's. I worried about my sexuality. I didn't have a girlfriend and didn't know if I even desired girls anymore. With Callahan, I imagined myself as a girl. I didn't even know what that meant; had no word for it, but feared I was some kind of homosexual. Yet I couldn't tell Callahan, who despised homosexuals. Increasingly I worried that I was having sex with him, even if he couldn't admit it. If that were the case, then he was innocent, and I was using him for my perversity.

Soon I broke out in acne. Huge boils developed on my cheeks and back, black swollen carbuncles pocked my chest. When I walked the halls at St. Mike's, the football players, cronies of the basketball seniors, slapped my shoulders and pounded my chest. At the time, I really didn't have a clue why. I didn't even realize they were trying to hurt me. Wasn't I a member of the team? If by chance someone fouled out, wouldn't they need me? At core, as intellectually precocious as I might have been, I was even more socially naive.

We played the last game of our regular season against Stuben East, with the winner claiming the city title. All that Friday during school St. Mike's rocked, with students chanting "Beat East! Beat East!" in the halls between classes and at a huge rally at the day's end. LaRuche and Dale brought the starting seniors onto the stage and everybody cheered. They were going to bring the title back to St. Mike's.

I hadn't been on the floor during a game in a month, and plagued with both acne and self doubt, I was bitter and depressed. But in all that time, in bed with Callahan, after the leg stretching and balls squeezing, after the hip pumping and Vaseline, lying in his arms, in the residue of my own sperm, Callahan had readied me for this moment. In fact, that evening before the game, in a ritual that would continue through my senior year, he'd exercised me and coached me in his bed. "The time will come," he said. "The time will come." Each of these bed sessions were meant to keep me physically and mentally prepared, living on the edge of that moment when I would be called on to perform. "You must live each moment on the bench like a man ready to step into battle," Callahan said. "You'll have to walk onto the floor and be ready. On. And ready. Tonight! Chuck Rosenthal, it will happen tonight! I can feel it. Be ready! It will be your moment. And you will seize it!"

That night, in front of a crowd of more than 5,000 standing-room-only fans in the Stuben Civic Auditorium, East broke out to a big early lead and held it. And despite having several starters in foul trouble, LaRuche stayed with them, afraid that a blown substitution would put him even more points behind. But down by seven with under four minutes to go, one of our forwards, our third leading scorer, fouled out. LaRuche put his face in his hands, then pulled at his short hair. He looked down the bench.

"Rosenthal!" he yelled.

"No," said Dale. "Try someone else."

"Who the hell else?" said LaRuche. "Rosenthal, are you ready?"

I was. I walked onto the floor under the silence of our despairing crowd. We were down by seven. East had the ball. And St. Mike's was stuck with me. Coming down the floor East immediately isolated their forward on me under the basket and passed him the ball. When he took a dribble I poked the ball from behind him and sent it to Feldon Richie who hit me streaking down the floor. I drove the left side and hit a scooping drive, left-handed, faking out East's star, Arlen Pooley, who had expected me to go back to my right hand.

Down the floor again East failed to score. When we came down, the ball came to me in the deep corner and I shot immediately, hitting again. Now East High went into a freeze, but I doubled down with Feldon Richie and we came up with a steal. The ball came to me in the deep corner again, but this time the zone came out to cover me. I faked a jumper, then dribbled left down the base line, took off on one side of the basket and came out with a reverse lay-up on the other, scoring and drawing a foul.

When I went to the line with the chance to tie the game with only seconds left, I heard the roaring for the first time. With almost no time left I could tie the game. Suddenly, the place was silent. Arlen Pooley walked up to me at the foul line and said, "Where the hell did you come from?"

"The bench," I said.

He put a low five on my hand. "I'm glad we're not playing your bench."

I hit the shot and sent the game into overtime.

In the overtime Feldon Richie and our center, Pete Powers, who'd kept St. Mike's in the game for the first three-and-a-half quarters, took the game out of my hands. I only touched the ball once in five minutes. We fell behind again. And even on our last possession, down by two with ten seconds left, Feldon dribbled down the floor and while I was open about twenty feet from the basket, he launched a thirty-five footer that missed by a mile.

After the game, LaRuche, Dale, and the whole football staff came into the locker room and shook my hand. I was too proud to be sad. In fact I believed that had they let me have the ball, I would have won the game for them. I didn't shower. I didn't even take off my uniform. I put my clothes on over my sweaty jersey and trunks and, like an idiot, did not walk home, but walked three miles through the bitter February night to Callahan's. He wasn't there. I poured myself vodka and orange juice and drank hard until he came home, exuberant with my success. I don't think he even noticed I was drunk.

We couldn't win our own city title but we won the state. Despite my performance that night against Stuben East, I never saw another minute of action until the last thirty seconds of the state title game, when we were up by thirty. Baffled and hurt, I ended my junior season. If I were anything but a confused child, I might have walked away from it all then.

But the summer brought the sun and hope. My acne melted away and Callahan went off to study. In the morning I walked downtown to the Y and played basketball, then hiked down to the dock and caught a ferry to the river beach. After a few hours of swimming, reading, and sun bathing, I took the ferry back to the dock and walked home where, on my backyard basketball court I'd find a dozen kids already playing: Avis and Darnel Wiley, Mikey Horton, Willie Warren, Leonard Seward, Arlen Pooley, and others, too. All black. And though I invited a number of my teammates from St. Mike's and friends, like Wooj, to come down and play, seldom did a white kid ever come to play on my court, and even then, only when there were no blacks.

Sam loved to see those kids there. He watched and kidded with the ones who were waiting for winners while Helen made orange Kool-Aid mixed with orange juice and brought it out to the back steps. We had those guys in for lunch and dinner and they had me over, too. Most often I visited Willie Warren who lived just a block away. The day Aubrey turned nineteen, we were all playing hoops in the yard when Helen invited everybody in for ice cream and cake. There must have been ten of us packed into the tiny dining room when Aubrey walked in with her boyfriend. "Well," said Aubrey. "Well. I wasn't expecting *this* for my birthday." Then we all sang happy birthday to Aubrey and ate ice cream and cake.

I didn't go to Columbus that summer and when Callahan returned and began the summer workouts at Holy Name, I invited my new friends. There was a quiet moment when I walked in the gym with them, but Callahan abided by his open door policy and let them play. Then, after a couple of weeks Callahan pulled me aside before a scrimmage.

"It's getting a little crowded with all these guys," he said.

"Let the alums play first. We'll pick up the winners."

"That's Y ball," he said. "Here we reward good play."

"That works, too," I said to him. "These guys trust you. Play the best ones. You don't have to change anything."

"I don't?" he said. He had his hand on his chin. He nodded slowly and turned away from me. But that night, after our therapy session, he brought it up again in bed-talk.

"Feldon and some of the others think the play is inferior," he said to me. "Showy and selfish."

"Black," I said.

He didn't respond.

"Say that to their faces," I said to Callahan. "Say it to mine."

Callahan himself was the one who only two years earlier had made me write essays, in the style of John F. Kennedy, Winston Churchill, Cicero, and Martin Luther King on a number of topics, among them, racism. I pointed that out to him.

"One must pick his battles," insisted Callahan. "You can't fight racism everywhere, every time."

"No, but we can fight it in our backyards and our gymnasiums," I said. "If Richie doesn't like the way my friends play, then let him field a team and play them. Best of seven."

Callahan rubbed his chin. "And who will you play with, Mr. Rosenthal?" he asked.

That problem was answered by Avis Wiley when I told my friends about the games.

"You play with the white guys," said Avis. "You're white."

"I'm one of you," I said.

"You're white," Avis said.

"When we kick their butts," said Arlen Pooley, "we don't want them saying it was because we had a white guy on our team. You play for them and get your ass kicked like a good white boy."

Hurt and conflicted, I played with the white team from Holy Name and St. Mike's.

"An interesting choice, Mr. Rosenthal," Callahan said to me before the game.

"I didn't make it," I said. "They did."

On that day Feldon Richie showed up with a team of white all-stars, including St. Mike's center, Pete Powers, now heading for Louisville on a basketball scholarship, and Clemson-bound Danny Hogan from Heart of Christ. Neither of those guys had ever played a minute at Holy Name before. I protested to Callahan who put up the palms of his hands, then I went over and apologized to my friends on the other end of the floor.

"Oh man, don't even worry," said Darnel Wiley, grinning.

In the end, Pete Powers was completely neutralized on the boards by burly little Mikey Horton, who hadn't even played in high school. And Arlen Pooley humiliated Feldon Richie that day, holding him scoreless and repeatedly taking him inside and muscling him or hitting a killer fade-away from distance. The blacks beat us badly and Callahan went over and shook all of their hands. "Excellent gentlemen," he told them. "Well played." Though he confessed to me that night that he was stunned. He simply never realized how much better a player Arlen Pooley was than Feldon.

The next game the white all-stars didn't show up, though neither did Arlen Pooley who told me that one game was enough, the point was proven. I led a group of Holy Name alums against my friends and a new ringer, all-city forward Taylor Tyson from Stuben Academy, where Avis and Darnel played. And though everybody had played at my house the night before, nobody'd told me about Tyson.

"You guys are pulling a fast one," I said to them.

"Oh, Taylor?" said Avis. "We just ran into Taylor on the way here. We needed somebody to play against you."

The game turned into a shoot out between me and Taylor. We were both red hot and neither could stop the other. By the second half, players on both teams were cheering us both. Even Callahan cheered when either of us scored. It was one of the best games I ever played. We won by one point and when it was done Taylor Tyson stood in front of me and looked me in the eyes. Then he walked away. That was all he did.

It was my neighborhood friends, not the Holy Name crowd, who gathered around me and hugged me after the game. "That was the future," Avis said to me. "Taylor was seeing the future."

The great white vs. black series died a natural death after that game. The argument about superior and inferior styles of play was dead. On a summer day, on a small, grade school basketball court, in a little city in southeast Ohio, a group of blacks and whites shook hands and, at least for a little while, forgot about the whole thing.

Maybe a little something was learned on both sides. My friends continued to visit and play at Holy Name even after I left, and became a recruiting force for Holy Name as other, younger blacks began to visit the gym. Years later, when Holy Name's inner-city, Catholic population base began to fade, the school successfully recruited young, non-Catholic black kids from my neighborhood, a strategy that kept the dynasty afloat for another decade.

After the series Callahan went out of his way to bring my neighborhood friends into the fold, even offering them scholarships to St. Mary's. Only Avis, who wanted to become an illustrator, accepted, but he didn't last long. He ended up working the streets, dealing drugs. Darnel joined the army and died in Vietnam. Mikey Horton took a job at G.E. Willie married several women and got in trouble for it, though when his little brother, Arpie, got arrested for holding up a gas station, my mother went to bat for him and served as his probation guide. After that, Arpie was all right. Leonard killed a man in a fight, went to jail, and then was murdered himself. Arlen Pooley won a basketball scholarship to Ohio U., then came back to Stuben College where he played basketball for two years. He went to work in the black community at the Martin Luther King Center.

That fall of my senior year there were race riots in Stuben that reached the high schools. At Stuben Academy, Darnel Wiley hit Herbie Thomas with a chair. The next day he showed up at Holy Name, found Herbie, and apologized. And if a block away cars were overturned and grocery stores put to flames, on a small court in my backyard we played basketball together. We hugged and joked and sweated. We played basketball.

Chapter Nineteen

That spring after my junior year Callahan put me in charge of the after-school and weekend intramural program at Holy Name. Working under Neal O'Donnel, who I now often saw drinking at Callahan's, I assigned teams and coaches, did the scheduling, and published a weekly paper with box scores and standings. I loved running that league.

Holy Name's basketball program had become so deep in talent that the seventh grade team now played their own schedule and the J.V. had two teams in the city league, O'Donnel's, made up of the first twelve, front-line fifth and sixth graders, the Red Team, and another, the Gold Team, made up of developmental players from the third to sixth grade. As a third grader, my brother Joe played on the Gold Team. Callahan made my dad the Gold Team's coach. Sam loved it, though he hated developing players and then giving them up to the Red Team.

Callahan brought in some friends of his, colleagues from St. Mary's who once coached high school football in Cleveland, and soon Holy Name's football program had turned around, too. He hung banners in the gym, listing every city title in football and basketball, a long list, and he hung State Championship banners listing the names of each player on the title teams. One year, when Holy Name lost the state title game, Callahan canceled a celebration that the school had planned for the team, win or lose. "No," said Callahan, "at Holy Name we do not celebrate almost winning. We do not celebrate defeat." When told that only one team could win it all, Callahan responded, "That's right. And only one team should celebrate." He laughed and threw his hands in the air. "That's why it's called a championship!"

At St. Mary's, where Helen was his executive secretary, for all practical purposes she ran the academic logistics of the college. That year Callahan came to our house for dinner; a tense enough affair, but everyone behaved, even Aubrey who said she hated Dan. Helen served fried catfish and mashed potatoes, something that was pretty popular locally when you could still get it fresh from the river. For us it was a big deal. It wasn't spaghetti, or chicken soup made from wings and necks; it wasn't out of a can; it wasn't day-old bread and instant gravy which was actually one of my favorites because I always got my fill. Callahan was jovial, but he picked at his food. He left in his usual way, telling my parents how proud they should be of all of us, how great they looked—they never seemed to age, he said—what great food. But I knew he was shocked by how poor we still were. Later in the week he tried to give us his old TV, but Sam turned him down.

"Why won't he let me help?" Callahan said to me.

"Pride," I said.

"Your family needs help," said Callahan. "It's nuts."

"Then it's nuts," I said.

"Aren't they both working?" he said.

"Give my mother a raise," I said.

"She's a secretary. I can't give college money away."

But that Christmas Eve after midnight mass, Callahan showed up on our porch at 1:30 in the morning with a baked ham. And he guaranteed a scholarship for Sylvie to attend St. Mary's. We were indebted to him, all of us, though sometimes Sam cursed his interference when he wasn't thanking him. And Helen held him accountable for my leaving the Church. What bothered them most was the late nights I spent out with Callahan, as late as two a.m., even on school nights. But they tried hard to weigh their protests against the advantages we'd all gained. Most often they were accepting, but when we fought, we fought about the same things over and over.

Not too long later Helen quit her job at St. Mary's to become the executive secretary to the Diocesan Director of Parochial Schools. She took me aside to tell me she was quitting. We sat in the dining room, her conference room, her prayer place, under the Virgin Mary. She was pretty gray now and in her mid-forties, but still very statuesque, her eyes full of both wonder and worry.

"It's more money, more work—I'll have to work Saturday mornings—more prestige."

"That's great," I said.

"I wanted to run it by you, because you're so close with Callahan."

"You think it will bother him?"

"He's powerful," she said. I could see she was trying to measure her words, but as always she was helplessly frank. "He rewards his friends."

"You're his friend," I said.

"And," she searched for the word, "*protects* himself from his enemies. That makes him a little manipulative," she said. "And sometimes duplicitous."

"The white lie," I said.

"White lies. Okay," said Helen. "I know he does a lot of good. I've seen it, with you, with us, and others. But sometimes he steps on people to get things done. People love him, and hate him, too, for good reasons."

"I get it, Mom," I said.

"As his right hand, sometimes I have to stand in front of him. I deal with the enemies all of the time. I feel vulnerable." She took my hand. "Chuck, I don't want to be there anymore when the shit hits the fan."

And Helen made her exit. Callahan told her that she was the best secretary he ever had. He shook her hand and told her to always let him know if he could be of any help in her new job. Later he told me she'd been rigid with those who worked under her, and inflexible. I shrugged at him. I said, "News."

Callahan took control of St. Mary's when it was on the verge of going under and convinced the nuns who ran the school to go coed. Then he introduced a police science program and a hotel-restaurant management program. He brought the little school exposure and alumni cash by instituting athletic programs in basketball, soccer, hockey, tennis, baseball, crew. From his position as Dean, he ran the school. Night after night, as I sat in his living room drinking, Callahan worked into the morning hours on schedules and budgets, plans for a new student union, indoor tennis courts and new dorms, building for the future of St. Mary's. Anyone who knew him well also knew that the unreachable, always-busy godfather of St. Mary's could be reached at his home between midnight and three a.m. where he'd be up, working, though often that work involved my therapy.

During those odd morning hours, important people from all over the city and even the state, called or visited, asking for help, advice, favors. Callahan worked the phone, made contacts, contracts, treaties. Word was that from behind the scenes he was the most influential man in the city. Callahan scoffed at that. "I run a small college in a small town," he laughed. "If I walked away tomorrow, everything I've done would be rubbed out in a year. People forget. They are fickle and petty, as greedy as they are good-hearted. For most people, the question is not 'What have you done for me?' but 'What have you done for me lately?'" Regardless, when those people showed up at the Dean's office, Helen wasn't in front of them anymore.

Returning no starters from our state championship team, my senior season began as a rebuilding year. Along with me and our center, Barry Novaczek from St. Pete's, we started a junior and two sophomores. We slaughtered a tiny school in our opener and I fouled out and scored only six points, but in our second game, out in the boondocks of West Virginia, I had forty-four. My parents, who'd driven down with Joe and Andy, were elated, but Callahan worried that the *Stuben Times* gave me so little attention. "You're unorthodox and unknown," he said at our next session. "You can't let up for a minute."

One of the sophomores, Ricky France, turned out to be sensational and we headed into a Christmas tournament at Hamilton High undefeated with Ricky and I both averaging over twenty. There, we beat the Michigan state champions in the first round and routed Hamilton on their home court in the final. But LaRuche left our starters in too long. Hamilton's subs took Ricky out on a drive to the basket, breaking his ankle. Worse news for me, though Ricky and I led the tournament in scoring, I didn't make the all-tournament team. I cried. Freddy Dale sat down next to me in the locker room.

"We're undefeated," he said. "We won the tournament. You should be ashamed of yourself, behaving like this."

"I've sacrificed everything for this," I said to him. "You know that."

I sat up straight and we stared at each other; Freddy Dale's dark, brown eyes offering me nothing. It was deeper than a lack of sympathy. It was hate.

"Each coaching staff got only two votes for their own team," Dale said to me. "Ricky was unanimous. I voted for Novaczek because of defense and rebounding. LaRuche did, too. We weren't the only ones. Think about it. You're too selfish." When he walked away I thought about it. Apparently the shit was falling now, and I was standing too close to the fan.

In our first city league game without Ricky, Stuben West collapsed on my inside driving game and we were beaten. Dale, and Novaczek too, complained that I wasn't distributing the ball, though LaRuche only complained that I didn't score enough when it counted. At night, alone in St. Mary's gym, Callahan taught me a jump-set shot so I could score from even farther away from the basket. I scored more. We lost again, to Stuben Tech. Dale fumed. He told me I was a liability. I was seventeen. And confused.

"Tell me what to do," I said to LaRuche. He recited a poem to me about how to bear when you were an anvil and strike when you were a hammer. "So what am I now?" I said.

"The hammer," said La Ruche.

But I was convinced that I could not play basketball without Callahan's therapy. Before every game I drank and slept with him. Then, before our third city game, against East, tired of the routine, tired of everything, and contemplating telling Callahan that I no longer wanted to take therapy, to play basketball, to do any of it, I went home after school, ate dinner with my family and took a nap. That night I played miserably and was held to only nine points in a defeat that drove us to the cellar of the city standings.

"Your failure was all over the news. Let that be a lesson to you," Dan Callahan said to me. "You're a slow starter. Too slow. You need to be warmed up. Don't risk another game like that. It could cost you All-City."

I stuttered something. I wanted to tell him then that I was sick of it all. As much as I wanted to be a star, I also wanted to be, as he would have said, nothing. And as dependent as I was on him, I wanted to get away. "You won't be there in college," I said.

"Suit yourself, Mr. Rosenthal," said Dan Callahan. "Suit yourself."

But only one suit fit. The next game, at home against Hamilton, I went to him, but after my therapy we both fell asleep. He rushed me to the game, but I arrived at the end of warm-ups, getting to the floor as the buzzer sounded to begin the game.

LaRuche was enraged. "Where the hell have you been?" he screamed. Callahan pulled him aside and Freddy Dale pulled me. "You've had it," Freddy said. "This is the last straw. You've had it."

I wondered how many straws I'd used up. I was unaware I'd been using up so many straws.

"Sit down!" yelled LaRuche. "You're benched! You might never start again!"

When the starting line-ups were announced, my back-up, Muley Henson, got a standing ovation. The others starters hugged him wildly. I sat on the end of the bench, miserable and befuddled. I'd just been in bed with Callahan. Now I was on the end of the bench with the fans roaring their approval for my substitute. Somewhere, things had gone very wrong.

Freddy Dale plopped himself down next to me to explain. "You're single-mindedness has ruined this team," he said. "You're all offense. You don't play any defense. That's why they're all cheering for Muley. You're a liability. Now this! We'll just see how important you are!"

After the first quarter we were down by eight; early in the second, by twelve. Novaczek got in a jump ball under our basket and LaRuche yelled down the bench.

"Rosenthal!" he said.

"No!" yelled Freddy Dale. "Stick to your guns. You said he wouldn't play!"

"I said he wouldn't start!" yelled LaRuche. "Get in there! Quick!" LaRuche said to me.

I went in for Muley who hadn't scored. The place was pretty quiet, except that my parents clapped. You don't really hear the crowd during a game, but when there are only a couple people clapping it tends to stand out. I walked to the top of the key. The referee threw the ball in the air and Novaczek controlled it, tipping it to me. I shot and scored. That game I sank everything I touched. I scored twenty-seven points in twenty minutes. We won by twenty-five. I was mobbed after the game.

"Great game!" Freddy Dale said, shaking my hand. "Great defense!"

"Thank you," I said.

One of the football coaches put an arm around me. "Glad to see you're out of your slump," he said.

"Slump?" I said.

After that, LaRuche just turned me loose. He moved me to point guard and let me pick up the best opposing guard in our man-to-man defense. Backing away from Dale, LaRuche made me the center of the offense. After I got the ball up the floor, I passed off and ran over any number of screens to get free for my fade-away jumper. But zones were my favorite because I could just plant and bomb. We righted ourselves, and going into our last city game against East, with a win we would tie them for the title.

Before each game I went to Callahan. Even for away games. At St. Mike's, athletes had the last period of school free so we could start practice, and my friend, Fr. Dee, who was aware of my sinus problems, let me leave school on the days of away games so I could get Callahan's therapy before coming back and getting on the bus. Unknown even to Callahan, when I was at his place I filled my flask, because I drank to get in bed with him and I drank after I got out. However warmed up I became from the therapy, I inevitably played with a buzz.

I don't know how implicitly Dee understood Callahan's therapy, but near the end of basketball season he was picked up by the police for soliciting boys down at the Stuben Train Station, a place known for homosexual interludes.

Callahan broke it to me in his bedroom. "Your friend, Fr. Dee, won't be back," Callahan said to me. "Did you know about him and boys?"

"He never touched me," I said. "Not once."

"My God, the train station," said Callahan. "How degrading."

"He kept it away from school," I said.

"How do you know?"

"I just know," I said. "Besides, it's his own business."

"What," said Callahan, pulling me down by the hair, "homo-sexuality?"

"What was he doing that was so bad?" I pushed. "Blow jobs? What?"

Callahan studied me. He shoved me down, then sat up and turned away, sitting on the edge of the bed. "You're an innocent boy, Chuck Rosenthal. You obviously know nothing about it."

In that way it was an odd winter. In his third year as J.V. coach, Neal O'Donnel lost a half-dozen games and failed to win the title. Neal was a sweet, almost sheepish, tough guy, but introspective and bright. He drank heavily. Often he went out to dinner and movies with Dan, like I did, and Wooj, and sometimes I found him drinking in Callahan's living room. After his losing season, he seemed to be drinking more. I didn't see O'Donnel out with Dan anymore and when I asked Callahan about O'Donnel, he said it looked like he'd have to fire him. It wasn't the losses, Callahan said, so much as the drinking. O'Donnel was one of those classic, Irish bachelor drunks. He'd been seen drunk in bars all over town. Then he lost his day job and Callahan fired him as J.V. basketball coach. Not too much later O'Donnel was entrapped and arrested in Youngstown for soliciting sex from a male prostitute.

Not a word was said about it at Holy Name. Dan Callahan shook his head. "Unbelievable," he said. "Who would have thought it?"

I might have, but I wasn't capable, and I was in the middle of a title drive as Larry LaRuche prepared us for our final game against Stuben East, a game with the championship on the line. LaRuche changed the offense, letting our off-guard bring the ball up the floor, then running me off double picks for my fade-away, or clearing out the floor entirely to let me go one-on-one to the basket. We changed our defense, too, going to a zone to counteract East's superior quickness. The *Stuben Times* made a big deal over the showdown. Darkhorse St. Mike's against perennial power East High. My offense against East's swarming defense. They'd stopped me cold last time, holding me to nine, but could they do it again? "Yes!" said Callahan. "Yes! You will be a legend." This was the game, and the game plan, I'd lived for. The chance to vindicate myself, to bring St. Mike's the city basketball championship.

But it didn't turn out that way. Though I scored a bundle, East swamped us by twenty. Even that went unreported because the next day the *Stuben Times* went on strike.

A few days later, playing dismally, we were beaten in the first round of the state tournament. The season was over. Until then,

I'd tried to ignore the fact that no college had recruited me for a basketball scholarship. Now Callahan told me not to worry. In a week the balloting would be done and I'd be on the Ohio All-State Team. The letters would come. But I didn't make All-State. I didn't even make first team All-City. And Barry Novaczek got the MVP award for St. Mike's.

I stood in Callahan's living room, my second string All-City notification in my hand. I was not a champion. I was not All-City. I didn't have a single college inquiry.

"Over twenty a game!" he exclaimed. "How could they ignore it! After all I've given up for you."

"After all you've given up," I said.

"It's not over yet, Mr. Rosenthal," said Dan Callahan. "It's not ever yet. Now get upstairs."

I didn't say anything to him. I just turned away and left.

Chapter Twenty

The next day I was back in the gym. "When you are not practicing," Callahan had once said, "somewhere, someone is, and
when you meet, he will beat you." I thought I had nothing else.
I played basketball. In hope and in despair, I played basketball.
I got into Cornell, Virginia, and Georgetown, but I'd have to
walk on to try out for basketball and needed a lot of financial
help to afford any of them.

Then Callahan convinced me to take a trip with him fifty miles
south to a nearby small college, Manfred, a Division III basketball
school on the West Virginia border.

"They haven't had a winning season since before I was born,"
I said.

"They're a good school. They've turned around their football
and baseball programs," said Callahan. "Look at they're schedule:
NYU, Chicago, Washington-St. Louis, Rochester."

"Wheelton," I said. "Thiel."

"They're making money available for athletes. What's more,
you'll play, maybe as a freshman."

I brought my gear and scrimmaged with some of the team as
the coach, a short, dapper man named Arnie Cox, watched. I played
well. Manfred hadn't had a winning season in eighteen years.

The next day Arnie Cox called my home. "I want you," he said.
"But we don't give athletic scholarships. You'll have to fill out a
financial aid form for an academic grant. And apply for admis-
sion, too."

He mailed me the forms with addressed and stamped return
envelopes and Helen helped me fill them out that day, though an
administatror from the school called before I even mailed them.

"Have you mailed in the applications?" the administrator said to my mother over the phone.

"Yes," said Helen, handing me the forms and pointing me out the door to the mailbox.

"Good," said the administrator. "I'm pleased to inform you that your son, Chuck, has a full academic scholarship to Manfred College."

Twenty-one

The summer before college, still seventeen, I began dating a friend of Sylvie's, Annie Silko. We spent our time laughing and talking, taking walks along the river. Things weren't like they were with Sally Thomas, but it felt soothing and normal to have a girlfriend. I was so inexperienced, and now fearful, that I talked to Callahan about necking and petting.

"What do you do?" I said.

"About what?"

"I want to touch her breasts."

"It's easy," he said. "I'll show you."

That night we practiced touching a girl's breasts. I practiced on him. French kissing and then moving down his neck to his shoulders until I finally put my head on his breast, then my hand, later kissing down until I sucked on his nipple. We did it over and over before we went into our usual routine. But when I went back to Annie, my stomach turned; I couldn't do it. I couldn't transfer it. So we necked and she rubbed on me. But when I told Callahan, because I told him everything, he said I shouldn't let her rub on me while necking unless I was going to get off, too. If she was rubbing on me, she was using me to masturbate.

"That's cool, I guess," I said.

"It's not," said Callahan. "You're not there just for her sexual satisfaction. What about yours?"

But by then I didn't think I could get excited enough to come with a girl. Once I started kissing, I imagined myself *as* a girl. As much as I liked Annie, I didn't really desire her and was happy that I got hard around her at all. Though there were other girls that summer, too, by luck and accident. During one summer party, I got drunk with a blonde from Hamilton and we necked furiously into the night. I was so excited that afterward I hounded her on the phone until she finally went out with me and I immediately told her that I loved her. She fled.

During my first month of college, autumn 1969, I came home every weekend, dated Annie and slept with Callahan. Then I met Rory Gore. At six-eight, Rory Gore was huge and fluid. He moved like a dancer. He spouted absurd, nihilistic philosophies. He'd been to Woodstock. Handsome and confident, with a mop of long, floppy, black hair, he womanized constantly and succeeded often. I met him near midnight on the first night of orientation where I saw him, a huge figure, carrying cement blocks from the construction sight of the new student union to the sidewalk of the quad.

"What are you doing?" I asked him.

"I'm building a wall, of course," he said. "It's nice of you to ask."

"About the wall?"

"Most people are afraid. Want to help?"

"Build a wall?"

"Yes."

"Why?"

"Everyone says they hate them, but they really love them," he said. "The Berlin Wall. The Great Wall of China. 'Something there is that doesn't love a wall.' Frost always said opposite things at once, don't you think? Everyone will love this wall."

So I lugged cement blocks and we built a wall about seven feet tall and some twenty feet long, right in the middle of campus. In the hour that it took us, a few people walked by but, as Rory Gore predicted, if we just went about our business with authority, nobody would say a thing. And nobody did.

The next morning the campus was buzzing and a picture of our wall appeared in the local newspaper and later in the week in the campus paper. But Rory never celebrated or gloated. In fact, he never said a word about the incident to me again.

I fell in with his crowd: Bob Angel, Chicken Thief, Meester Meester, Freak, and Flaming Joe from just outside Pittsburgh who, together with Rory, ordered dozens of cupcakes from a bakery on Saturday nights and sold them at inflated prices in front of the cafeteria on Sunday mornings. They squiggled a line in the frosting and sold them as Flaming Joe's Egyptian Cupcakes with a Carving of the Ohio River on Top. "There's a carving of the Ohio

River on each one," Flaming Joe from just outside Pittsburgh told every customer, pointing to the frosting. "See?"

Rory and I took to each other like magnets. We sat gabbing at each other deep into the morning hours. We drank beer and hard liquor. Bob Angel scored some pot and took Rory and me out into a field behind the dorm.

"Are you afraid?" said Bob.

"Should I be?" I said.

"I don't know," he said. "I've never smoked pot."

"Rory?" I said.

"Nope," said Rory.

"You didn't smoke pot at Woodstock?"

"I smoked a peace pipe at Woodstock," said Rory.

"He wasn't at Woodstock," said Bob Angel.

"I was somewhere," Rory said.

"He was at Slippery Rock," said Angel.

"I was aiming for Woodstock," said Rory Gore.

As if we needed pot. We shared a joint, then another. We sat looking at each other.

"Let's get drunk," said Rory.

Not long after that, Freak, who wore bell bottoms and had long hair and a beard, and Flaming Joe got some *real* stuff, laced with opium. Expecting much of the same as our first experiment, this time the five of us sat stunned. Time stretched and shrank. When we tried to walk, the floor turned rubbery, the dorm hallway waved like a noodle. We howled. Cried. Laughed. When we woke up in a pile of ourselves in the morning, Flaming Joe said, "Whew, that was scary. Let's do it again." And we did. A lot.

I stopped going home on weekends. I stopped seeing Annie. I phoned Callahan. When I told him about the opium he exploded at me. "You'll kill yourself," he said. "That was no dabbling, that was a drug trip. Those are dangerous drugs. I want you to promise never to take any drugs, ever again, or I'm through with you for good. Promise me," he said.

"I promise," I said.

I hung up and dropped LSD. We took mescaline and ate mushrooms. One night, on LSD, Rory tried to convince me to climb five stories of scaffolding and onto the steel girders of the unfinished student union.

"I don't want to fly," I said. "I'm not like Art Linkletter's daughter."

"Who's talking about flying," laughed Rory. "I'm talking about walking." He spread his huge arms and strode. His flushed face beamed.

"I'm afraid of heights," I said.

"Why?"

"Why? Because they're high," I said. "You can fall off. I don't want to know what I'd be thinking on the way down."

"You can't fall off," said Rory Gore. "You can't fall off a mountain. That's Gary Snyder."

"I don't know Gary Snyder. I don't trust Gary Snyder."

"Look," said Rory. "Look down now. We're walking on a sidewalk. Have you ever fallen off a sidewalk?"

"How could you fall off a sidewalk?" I said.

"Exactly!" said Rory. "You can't fall off a sidewalk. And you can't fall off a steel girder. Don't fall off of it, just walk on it."

At the time it made sense. We climbed the scaffolding and out onto the girders at the top of the building, staring down five stories through space. We sat atop the structure, legs dangling, drank bourbon and smoked pot. I had no urge to jump or fly or fall off. I felt cemented to the steel. Rory slapped my back. "Ah-ha, my friend," he said. "Death is nothing. And we are immortal. Bound by testing the edge of excess."

"Death is everything and we are mortal," I said.

"Exactly," said Rory.

"Death is the end," I said.

"Of what?" said Rory. "Death is the beginning."

"Of what?"

"Some things end, others begin."

"What begins when I end?" I said.

"Something else," Rory Gore said. "Begin, end, begin. Some things end, others begin. Which would you rather emphasize? Begin, of course."

We broke into the chapel and played the campus chimes at three in the morning. Broke into the science building and played with the planetarium. Broke into the chemistry lab and mixed concoctions. Our favorite break-in was the basement swimming pool in the old sports complex. After practice we left a locker room window cracked open, then, around one a.m., crawled over some pipes above a culvert, pried open the window and slipped in. After jimmying a few door locks with a student I. D. card, we had the whole old dark swimming pool to ourselves.

Manfred College hadn't had a winning basketball season in eighteen years, but our freshman class was loaded with talent. In our first scrimmage with a nearby college, the varsity got lambasted. In the following scrimmage against their freshmen, we won big. After the scrimmage, Arnie Cox moved me up to varsity.

Rory played basketball carelessly. As in life, his passion was hit-and-miss, his play imbued with misplaced joy and desireless grace. In cosmic terms, he had the perfect attitude. Athletically, he was a flake. "People are dying in Vietnam," Rory said to me once on the sidelines, "and I'm supposed to take this seriously?"

"While you're doing it," I said.

"There's an idea," said Rory Gore.

It was a miserable program. We didn't play a real game until January. But the varsity practiced two weeks into Christmas vacation, staying in an old frat house, and returned to practice for two more weeks, double sessions, the day after Christmas. As miserable as it was, I felt glad to be away from Callahan who I talked to on the phone and saw only briefly during my short break.

"You seem to be enjoying college life," he said to me in his living room.

"Yes," I said.

"Have you been exposed to any more drugs?"

"No," I said.

"Whatever else you do, if you take drugs I'll never speak to you again," Dan Callahan said. "Now get upstairs. I don't see you as often, it's important to keep you nimble."

To keep me nimble. He did it for me. But I felt beyond it now. I knew it was sex. Sex that he couldn't admit he was having with me, and I surmised a number of others. And though he could not say it, I believed that I was his favorite and that he loved me deeply as a friend. I loved him. And for all he had given me and for all he would give, I slept with him out of love, though I had developed a distaste for it, in fact I despised it and I had for some time.

Back at Manfred, two nights into the after-Christmas, double practices, Rory and I sneaked out of the frat house and broke curfew. We walked downtown to the local bars where, despite being well under-age, Rory usually convinced most bartenders to serve us, partly because of his amiability and partly because of his size. When one bartender said, "no," Rory put a huge fist in his face and held it there.

"You think you're going to intimidate me with that?" the guy said.

"Yes," said Rory Gore.

He sold us a six-pack, as long as we promised to leave. We took the beer and broke into a dorm, drank, smoked pot, and watched TV in the lounge. We talked. We talked incessantly. Rory Gore filled my ears with Buddha and Nietzsche, Marx and Engels, Jim Morrison and Marquis de Sade. It turned out that but for Morrison, he knew little about any of them, but he knew enough to excite me. We did this until we were caught by a security guard on the last night.

Arnie Cox was furious. "How long have you been doing this?" he said.

"Just tonight," said Rory.

"We were exhausted," I said. "We needed a break."

He ordered us to clean the frat house after everybody left. But after everybody left, we did, too.

Rory and the freshman team won all of their games, played before the varsity games, all of them played in front of nobody. By the end of January the varsity was 0–10. I sat the bench. I begged Cox to either put me back on the freshman team or play me.

"I don't want you tired in case I decide to use you," Cox said to me.

"You don't use me," I said.

"These juniors and seniors have given me three good years. They're my friends."

It was true. They liked each other. They didn't call him coach, but Coxie or Arnie

"They've given you three crummy years, Coach," I said.

"There's more to life than winning," said Cox. "Though you might not think so. We're trying to have fun. And those guys deserve my loyalty."

"Why did you offer me a scholarship?"

"You have an academic grant based on financial need," he said to me. "You looked like you'd fit in."

"Losing is not fun," I said.

"Look at what's happening around you," said Arnie Cox. "The campus is inflamed with the anti-war movement. There's a complete change coming. In ten years there won't be any fraternities or intercollegiate athletics. It will be over. No one comes to our games. No one cares."

"Because we lose."

"You have a bad attitude," said Arnie Cox.

Rory thought I should leave Manfred College and play in Division I, but there were good reasons why I didn't think I could. If I could hit twenty jump shots in a row, and I could, I also often shot on the run, off the wrong foot, and fading away from the basket. If I'd practiced constantly to be able to hit jumpers, jump hooks, running hooks, and drives, right and left handed, if on a good day I could dunk, I was also awkward and unpredictable. Playing a lot of backyard ball against talented, big kids, I'd learned to release my shots either earlier or later than my defender expected. I could release my jump shot on the way down, my driving hook by swinging the ball behind my head after I was past the backboard. It was the kind of stuff that drove coaches nuts.

Worse, I had no confidence. I sat on the toilet before every game and poured out my bowels from the fear that if I got in I wouldn't play well. For all that Callahan had done for me, I now believed that I could do nothing without him.

As we faded winless into our nineteenth losing season, the pressure mounted on Cox to win. Arnie Cox finally put me in at Lehigh with two minutes to go. I had two steals and scored eight points. In the last ten minutes against Oberlin, I scored thirteen.

"Yeah, but you took twenty shots," said one of the seniors.

Somebody had to do it. Sometimes I scored a point a minute and sometimes I did shit. Cox started me the next game at Gettysburg and I scored only six.

At 0–16, with NYU coming in to Manfred, Cox finally folded to the pressure and started an all-freshman team. I called my parents and Callahan, too, and they all came down for the game.

Even Rory was excited. We smoked pot and listened to the Stones' "Sympathy for the Devil," then danced down to the gym. And we led at the half. Our two hundred fans stood and applauded as we left the court. Then, in the second half, Cox played his upperclassmen. As the lead evaporated, the small crowd began to boo. Rory stood up at the end of the bench and spread his huge arms. "Arnie," yelled Rory, "my friend. You're blowing it." Behind him, several fans cheered Rory and jeered Arnie Cox.

Cox stood and strode to Rory Gore, his forehead barely as high as Rory's chest. "Sit down, my friend," he said.

Arnie Cox was committing career suicide.

After the defeat, Callahan stormed down from the bleachers. He put a finger in Cox's face. "You're an idiot!" he yelled. "An incompetent idiot!" Cox looked at him sadly, put his head down, and walked away.

We stopped practicing after that. Cox just threw a ball on the floor and let us pick up sides. In the next eight games he played us freshman more and we won four of them.

"I shouldn't have yelled at him like that," Callahan said to me later. "I was just so enraged by his stupidity."

"He's actually a bright man. Too bright and sensitive to coach," I said, though I did not like Cox and he didn't like me.

"What a load of baloney," said Dan Callahan. "If he doesn't want to coach, he should find something else to do."

Cox did. He quit coaching to take an administrative position in Beirut.

Despite my frolicking with Rory and the boys, I'd managed to keep my head in the books and pull *B*'s. In fact, college was pretty easy. If you showed up for class and read the assignments you were doing more than almost everybody but the eggheads. And like Callahan, my mentor, I thought I'd major in history. Though one course I struggled in that winter term was Astronomy and if it hadn't been for Rory Gore, who broke the hatch door to our dorm roof and taught me the constellations and the movements of the moon, planets, and stars, I might not have passed. Of course, he seldom went to class, but the night before the final he stayed up with me all night and taught me everything.

"How do you know all this stuff?" I asked him. We stood on the roof of our dorm, our breath puffing into the dark air and the late winter stars bejeweling the black sky.

"When I heard the learned astronomer," said Rory Gore. "When the proofs, the figures, were arranged in columns before me; when I was shown the charts and diagrams, to add, divide, and measure them; when I sitting, heard the astronomer where he lectured with much applause in the lecture room, how soon unaccountable I became tired and sick, till rising and gliding out I wandered off by myself, in the mystical moist night-air, and from time to time, looked up in perfect silence at the stars."

"No kidding," I said.

"Walt Whitman," said Rory Gore.

"Oh Captain, My Captain," I said.

"No shit," Rory Gore said.

The morning we got our grades I found him throwing snowballs near the old swimming-gym complex. He wasn't exactly throwing them near the building. One wall of the building was all windows in small, wooden frames and Rory was throwing iceballs at them.

Gigantic Rory Gore, his leg kicking out like a baseball pitcher, his long arms wangling in space, launched a snowball. Glass smashed. Though dozens of students scurried by him, no one said a word.

"My friend," I said to him, "you might be able to fool these others, but you can't fool me. I see you're throwing snowballs at windows."

"Ah-ha!" said Rory Gore. "But you're wrong. I'm throwing snowballs at those icicles hanging from the roof."

In fact, there was a long row of crystal icicles hanging from the gutter. Some of them hung down in front of the windows. He launched a snowball and hit one. It fell into the snow.

"You see?"

He threw another and smashed a window.

"I am throwing at the icicles, but I am often missing," he said. He reached to the ground and molded a ball of ice. He offered it to me on his palm. "Would you like to join me, my friend?"

"I don't have a very good arm," I said.

"Ah, but I do," said Rory. He smashed another window.

"You flunked something," I said to him.

"I flunked everything," said Rory Gore.

"Astronomy?"

"Astronomy."

"How the fuck did you flunk astronomy?"

"Did you get an *A*?" he asked.

"A *B*."

"The difference between you and me," said Rory Gore.

"You're going to get in trouble for breaking these windows," I said.

He hesitated, looked at me with widened eyes, then launched another. Crash. He let his arms fall to his sides, then lifted his right one and let it drop on my shoulder. "Let's you and I have a cup of coffee with vanilla ice cream," he said. "Then we'll take a lot of drugs. And tonight. Tonight! Ah-ha!" said Rory Gore. "Less thought, more wine!"

That night, together, we gazed again at the sky. I reevaluated success. And I reevaluated failure. Maybe I'd spent too much time in the gymnasium and not enough time looking up in perfect silence at the stars.

Twenty-two

———∞∞∞———

For the first time in five years I hadn't spent time with Callahan in months, but after the season he asked if I wanted to take a trip with him over spring break.

"It's been a tough year," he said to me over the phone.

"Another one," I said.

"What are you doing for spring break?"

"Rory's hitching to Florida."

"That's dangerous," said Dan Callahan. "What will you do for money?"

"I haven't thought it out."

"I'm taking a trip to the Bahamas with Wooj," Callahan said. "Want to come?"

"The Bahamas? Really?"

"Come on. I'm going to Nassau. Wooj will need a roommate. I'll pay for everything, as a reward for all your work."

Before that I'd never been anywhere outside Ohio except for my trips with Callahan to Washington and New York. We flew from Cleveland to Miami and then to Nassau. In the British Colonial Sheraton, Callahan stayed in one room, and me and Wooj in the adjoining suite. Callahan arrived a little woozy from the flying and barely nibbled at his steak dinner that night. When we got back to the hotel he went right to bed.

"Wooj," I said, "we've got the night to ourselves."

"Yeah, how about that," Wooj said. He rubbed his wide forehead with is thumb and index finger. "Unless he feels better later."

"Let's not be here. Let's go drinking."

"Oh, I don't know," said the Wooj. He was still a big, sweet kid. He didn't play organized basketball anymore. St. Mike's ruined that. And his grades had been too poor to end up anywhere but St. Mary's under Callahan's protection. But there we were, together in the Bahamas with Dan under the same binding and silent contract.

"Come on," I said. "Don't wait here."

"What if he needs us?"

"For what?" I finally convinced him. I bought a pint of rum from the hotel liquor store and we went into the balmy night and walked the rowdy streets; college kids everywhere, on the sidewalks drinking out of brown paper bags, hanging off the porches of bars. And girls. Everywhere girls.

In the morning Wooj and I woke up and took off for the hotel beach, then we walked downtown and ate beef brisket with a glass of Courage. It wasn't until the afternoon that Callahan joined us on the shore. He wore Bermuda shorts with his socks pulled up over his calves, a short-sleeve banlon shirt with dollar bills showing through the pocket. "That's how you get attention in a place like this," he said. He ordered us all some pineapple-rum drinks. He never took off his clothes or swam; I figured he was embarrassed because of his psoriasis.

"Finish up here, gentlemen" said Callahan. "Then we'll go out to dinner."

When we got back to the room, Callahan called the Wooj in while I showered. Wooj didn't have to stay nimble anymore, but he still had sinus trouble. That meant I'd get the night shift. Dan took us to a Japanese restaurant where a chef cooked steak and vegetables for us at the table. A new experience, said Callahan, to open our young minds. Then we walked along the same streets the Wooj and I had walked the night before. Callahan glanced at the partying college kids who roved the corners and hung from the outdoor bars. "Shameless," he said. But he loved the British shops and restaurants and the white uniformed police in their domed and visored white helmets. Then he took us to the shopping quad outside the hotel and let us pick out Hawaiian shirts, colorful cutoff shorts, new bathing suits. When we were done he told us to go out and have some fun, try to meet some girls. He told me he'd see me when I got back.

We didn't know how to meet girls, though I ditched the Wooj early and wandered to the Buccaneer, the wildest bar on the strip. Even the white-jacketed policemen smoked hashish there, standing at the bottom of the stairs, their faces black-blue under their white hats. I got good and stoned, then wandered back to the Sheraton where Callahan waited.

"Did you have a good time, Mr. Rosenthal?" said Dan Callahan, opening the door to his side of the suite. "Get plenty to drink?"

"I don't know how to meet girls," I said.

"In due time, Mr. Rosenthal," he said. "In due time." I took off my clothes and once again I was in his arms.

The next morning at the beach a round-faced, blond man pulled his chaise up next to mine. He was middle-aged and a little dumpy with white hair on his chest. He looked a good ten years older than Callahan. "Hello," he said. "Do you mind?"

"No," I said, though I was suspicious. Like any kid, like what I regarded as any normal kid, I was absurdly homophobic.

"Spring break?" he said to me.

"Yeah," I said.

"How lucky for you."

"Everybody gets one," I said.

"To be here, I mean." He had a lilt to his voice, and a precision to his speech. He moved his hands gently in front of him as he spoke. That meant fag to Wooj, who got up abruptly and headed for the water. Then a young man came up and stood next to my new acquaintance. He was slender and blond, and carried a small, blue and white bag over one shoulder. "I'm Owen," said my new friend, offering me a soft hand, "and this is Eric." But Eric stood there coldly, offering nothing.

"Going off?" Owen said to him. "Shopping?"

Eric nodded.

"Well buy me something," Owen said.

Eric walked away and Owen turned to me. "Your friend and my friend are both rather unfriendly, aren't they?" he said. "I teach film at the University of Toronto. Is your older friend a teacher?" When I said nothing he said, "I saw the three of you here yesterday. You're hard to miss."

"Basketball coach," I said. "But he teaches college."

"Americans, obviously," he said. "Eric is a Fin. I met him here. He's not as bad as he seemed. I'm sure you'd get along."

I felt a dozen conflicting things. Obviously there was a relationship between Owen and Eric, one I didn't really understand, or didn't want to understand. How could I dare understand it? That's why the Wooj was in the water, running away.

For the next two days Owen came and sat with me and talked about books or movies. Sometimes he touched me lightly on the arm or leg as we spoke.

"How can you stand that?" Wooj said to me later one day.

"Stand what?" I said.

"That queer touching you."

"What's he done?" I said. "He's not hurting me."

"He's a queer," said Wooj. "And he's touching you."

"But if he weren't queer," I said, "then it would be okay?"

"He's queer," said Wooj.

So while I conversed with Owen, Wooj ran off. Eric stood sullenly in the distance, then disappeared for an hour or two before coming back. Owen said good-bye and went off to meet him. Then Callahan came down, like clockwork, though he never said a word till after my third night of lonely carousing. He began to wrestle with me and as usual I played a passive, naked partner, because if I got the best of him, as I could now, he grabbed my hair or nuts, so why bother. I let him twist my leg up to my chin, pin my arm, so he could talk to me, his face a breath from mine.

"You have a new friend," he said.

"He's a professor," I said. "Like you."

"Indeed."

"University of Toronto."

"What do you think of his companion?" Callahan said.

"He never talks to me," I said. "He wears a purse."

"Lots of men carry bags in Europe," said Callahan.

"Are you saying he isn't queer?" I asked him.

He pushed me away a little, but held on to me. "I'm saying not to make hasty judgments."

"You hate queers," I said.

"I do not hate homosexuals," Callahan said with emphasis. "I abhor the homosexual lifestyle, effeminacy, flamboyance, promiscuity, and other things that you know nothing about."

"Tell me," I said.

"Tell you what?"

"About it."

"You're not ready, Mr. Rosenthal."

"What am I not ready for?"

"Believe me, Mr. Rosenthal, you're not ready."

But for sharing a beer at lunch, the Wooj and I had now pretty much gone our separate ways. I hung out with Owen on the beach in the mornings. In the afternoon Callahan came down and drank rum drinks with Wooj and me before taking us to dinner. Then there was the night. I went out alone. And returned alone, to Callahan. One morning Owen suggested that we all have dinner together, but Eric was busy and Wooj adamantly rejected it.

"Why don't you have dinner with Owen by yourself?" Callahan said to me.

"Don't you want to come?" I said.

"Wooj might feel left out," said Dan Callahan.

Owen had given me his room number. I didn't think to call him. A little frightened, and tempted, too, I walked down and knocked on his door.

"Well, hello," he said. "How surprising."

There in the doorway, before he could invite me in, I told him that Wooj felt uncomfortable and Dan didn't want to leave him out.

"How odd," Owen said.

"It would just be me," I said. "Eric wouldn't like that."

Owen watched me for a moment in silence. "Oh, he'd get over it," he finally said. It was almost a sigh. "But best we just drop it."

When I joined Callahan and Wooj on the beach for drinks, Dan laughed. "Decided to join your old friends, I see," he said. "Not feeling adventurous."

Wooj sneered.

I felt like a boy being eaten by a hundred invisible things.

That night I went out to the bars again, wandering eventually to the Buccaneer where I stood leaning my back on the smoky bar under the blast of rock music. I was a confused kid. I thought I'd just head back to the hotel, buy a pint of scotch and sit on a dock somewhere, watch the water, gaze through the clear aqua sea right down to the garbage. Then a guy tapped me on the shoulder.

"Want to meet a girl?"

"Don't you?" I said.

"Yeah," he said, "but she doesn't want to meet me. She wants to meet you." He pointed across the dance floor. A young woman sat in a chair. She wore a short, brown and black striped dress; one long, tan leg crossed over the other. Her thick, almost black hair fell straight over her shoulders. She had striking blue eyes. She offered me a drunken smile.

When I walked over to her, she didn't get up. She was gorgeous and she was pretty snockered. The music was loud, so I knelt down next to her on one knee and spoke into her ear. "You didn't really want to meet me," I said.

She laughed.

I said, "Do you want to dance?"

Like a miracle, the music went slow and I took her in my arms. We danced. We danced some more. Drank more. Smoked hash. When another slow song came up we danced again. And kissed. She said her name was Robin and she was a grad student from Chicago.

"How old are you?" she asked.

"Eighteen," I said.

"Jesus," she said, "I'm twenty-eight."

I was wild about her. And so proud. We left the Buccaneer together. I put my jacket over her shoulders and we walked and kissed. We caught a floor show at a hotel and drank vodka gimlets, then she took me by the hand and led me down to the public beach. Across the street was her hotel and we went up to her room. Next to her bed she let my jacket drop to the floor behind her and kissed me, pulling my shirt down from my shoulders, pulling me down onto the bed. She put her thigh between my legs and wrapped herself around me. I took her head in my hands and we french kissed. And then, somehow, I passed out.

She woke me in the morning and hustled me out.

"My roommate will show up," she said.

"So what?" I said, trying to kiss her, but she shoved me out the door.

"Call me," she said. "Call me later."

By the time I got back to the Sheraton, Wooj was already on the beach. Callahan was waiting in our room, reading the paper next to the bed.

He looked up. "Well, Mr. Rosenthal, she was a beautiful girl," he said. "Wooj and I saw you walk by last night."

"I passed out," I said to him. "I fell asleep."

He raised his eyebrows.

"I'm supposed to call her later."

"Really," he said. "You expect to see her again."

"Why not?" I said.

But after lunch she didn't return my calls. I called again and again, doggedly, until someone picked up. It sounded like Robin, but she said she was Robin's roommate. Robin was showering and would call me as soon as she got out. After waiting two more hours I realized the phone call wasn't coming. Then Callahan dragged me into his room and into his bed.

"I fell asleep," I said.

"But now your virginity is saved!" Callahan laughed. "Besides, she was just using you, Mr. Rosenthal. It was only going to be one night whether you fell asleep or not."

But I didn't believe that. I believed that had I made love to her, I'd still be there with her. I believed there was something wrong with me. Callahan pulled me to him. We wrestled. I came with all my virgin cum between his legs. And emerged from his room completely disgusted with myself.

That night I got drunker than I'd ever been in my life. I wandered from bar to bar, twice returning to the Buccaneer, but of course Robin wasn't there. I walked to the public beach and stood across from her hotel. I stood there and cried. I cried about the whole fucking mess. Back at the Buccaneer one more time, I stood at the bar, smoking hash and drinking straight whiskey until I could barely stand. Some time after two a.m. I staggered out and headed back to the hotel. Though I never made it. I fell in the street and passed out in the gutter.

Owen found me there. "My goodness," he said. "What have you done to yourself?"

"Got drunk," I said.

"You most certainly did," Owen said.

He helped me sit up, then put my arm around his shoulder and walked me to the hotel, then up to his room. "We don't want your friend, Mr. Callahan, to see you like this," he said. I was so plastered I could barely move. He lay me down on his bed, threw my arms over my head and pulled off my shirt. He took off my sneakers, then unzipped my shorts, tugging them down over my feet. I lay there then in only my jockey's under his gaze, under the incandescent light. As his eyes shifted over me, settling on my crotch, I thought, well, let's see what he does; let's see what homosexuals really do.

"You're quite gorgeous and quite drunk," Owen said. "I'm going to have to take off those shorts."

I shrugged. He reached down and pulled my shorts down over my legs. Now I lay naked in front of him. He raised an eyebrow and nodded. "The mystery unveiled," said Owen. "I can understand the attraction." Then he reached down, grabbed my wrist and pulled me off the bed. "Cold shower for you," he said. He led me into the bathroom and held me under the cold shower. "Feeling better?" he said as he dried me off. I grunted. He let me lay down again, naked on his bed. That's when Eric came in.

Eric stared at me, then walked stiffly to the other side of the room, opposite the foot of the bed.

"He's very drunk," Owen said to Eric.

Eric said nothing. I met his cold gaze.

"Oh Eric, he couldn't do anything even if he wanted," Owen said. He turned to me. "You have had blow jobs before," he said.

But by then I was a little more clear-headed and I felt the jig was up. "Yes," I said to him, "and I don't want one right now."

Owen laughed. Eric sneered. Then Owen helped me dress and took me back to my room where I stumbled to my bed and passed out.

In the morning Callahan pressed me hard for a recap of the events to see how they matched up with the story Owen told him the night before. Owen was pretty straight about it all, though he left out the parts about the shower and the blow job.

"He saw you naked," Callahan said to me. "Did you get hard?"

"I was really drunk," I said.

"You have tremendous girth, Mr. Rosenthal. Had he seen you erect, he might not have been able to resist."

"What are you talking about?"

"Mr. Rosenthal, you know nothing about homosexuals."

"Listen," I said to Callahan, "he was a perfect gentleman. He helped me. When I said that I didn't want a blow job he left me alone and brought me here."

"But you've never had a blow job, have you?" said Callahan.

"What do you mean?" I said.

"You've never had sex with a man."

"Maybe I have," I said quietly.

"You have no idea," said Dan Callahan. "If you had sex with a man, real homosexual sex, you'd know it."

But if I'd never had sex with a man, then I'd never had sex with anybody. Yet how was I different from Eric? How was Wooj different? Was I a homosexual prostitute? Or a virgin? I tried walking around myself to look at who I was, a boy on vacation with his ex-coach. My coach who gave me physical therapy. No. It was sex. I knew it, but Callahan didn't. So I did it for him because I loved him. Because he couldn't admit it, but he loved me. Or because I was afraid to give up trips like this, and food, booze, and clothes. Or because I feared I couldn't accomplish anything without him, that without him I would fall back into mediocrity and poverty and have no one to turn to for help. How could Callahan not know that we were having sex? What the hell was sex anyway?

I dream I am in a room with Dan. It is his house though it is not a house I recognize. The room is plush and very, very warm. Callahan is seated in a thickly upholstered, upright chair. He wears a silk, paisley smoking jacket. Unlike his true looks, he is very handsome and stately, more square-jawed with a full head of hair, yet somehow I also realize that he is balding and portly, his glasses awkwardly propped upon his oval face. There is a fire, and a mantle over the fireplace with candelabra and busts of famous men. The walls are thick, the carpeting thick. Everything about the room is oppressive.

I pace in front of Callahan. "You have sex with me," I say. "I'm just a boy."

Callahan speaks calmly. "I don't know what you're talking about," he says.

"We have sex!"

"No," he says. "No."

"I loved you!" I cry. "I trusted you!"

He knits his brow. He looks at me calmly. He says, "Trust?"

Where am I? I left my father's car parked near St. Mary's. But this campus is huge and reminds me of Ohio State. Suddenly I am in bed with Callahan. I feel him at my back, his scratchy chest and legs upon me, his beard at my neck. I'm afraid about staying to long. About getting Sam's car back to him so he can go to work in the morning. Callahan pulls my arm behind my back and his limp penis drops into my hand. I turn. I face him. "No," I say.

Callahan grabs my hair. He pins me down. He says, "You are not a man."

Twenty-three

Not long after getting back to school Nixon invaded Cambodia. As I attended my first protest, a peace rally in downtown Manfred Square, the National Guard murdered four students at nearby Kent State. When word reached us, one of the professors walked to the flagpole and lowered the American flag to half-mast. When the police stepped forward to arrest him, we surrounded him, shouting. There'd never been anything like it in quiet, little Manfred. The police backed away and hundreds of us stayed there under the flagpole all night.

In a week we'd shut down the campus. Rory Gore was seeing a willowy, black-haired woman named Anna and the three of us began hitching rides to protests at Kent State, as well as other colleges, rallies in Cleveland and D.C. In hostels and hippie houses and tents, those two made love while I gathered myself up in my sleeping bag. Once on campus and once downtown, in front of the justice building, the three of us were detained for lowering the American flag. There was no school. We smoked pot and dropped acid. I met Anna's roommate, Lola, and fell in love.

Times were fast. Things happened fast. Rory wasn't faithful to Anna, and if Rory could love a different woman every night and not care whether or not he left them the next day or they left him, then I was the opposite. I was crazy for olive-skinned Lola who was buxom, wild, and notorious. Within a week she tried to corner me every chance she got, but I was intimidated and in way over my head. She thought I was a hot shit and just playing coy, until one night, drinking wine in Rory's room with Rory and Anna, they left us alone. We necked. Lola tore off her clothes, then mine. I fingered her clumsily, then while I fumbled at her labia with my lips she grabbed me by the hair and yelled, "Will you just fuck me!" It was a little too direct. I wilted. She left.

I disappointed a couple more girls, but by the end of spring term I had a new girlfriend, Cameron Marney, who was a year older than me, though much closer to my speed. In the two weeks that I'd known her we necked and petted and rubbed, but we didn't make love. She was feminine, smart and pretty, with long, blonde hair. When with her, I aroused myself by imagining myself *as* her. When alone I did the same, masturbating twice a day. Frightened now that I was horribly abnormal, possibly dysfunctional, I drank more than ever, day and night. I took what drugs I could lay my hands on. I brooded. I was depressed. I worried that I could neither play basketball nor have sex without Dan Callahan and felt increasingly, fearfully, more dependent and more repulsed.

At the end of spring I lingered on campus until the last hour of expulsion from the dorms, then reluctantly let Sam bring me back to Stuben. I talked with him a little about Cameron Marney. Sam talked about coaching. He coached for Callahan now and Joe played for him. Sam complained a bit about how when kids got good, Callahan moved them off his team. If he couldn't keep the kids he developed, he'd never win.

"Well Sam," I said, "you're not supposed to win."

"You think he doesn't complain if I don't win?" Sam said.

"He doesn't pay you," I said.

"Not directly," said Sam.

Aubrey was finishing her third year at St. Mary's and next year would be Sylvie's first. I didn't have to worry too much about money. I had some left from my book and food stipend on my academic scholarship.

"I got the contract for the new science building up at St. Mary's," Sam said.

"Were you the lowest bidder?" I said.

"After I knew what the lowest bid was." He was quiet for a while. We were doing a lot better. Helen was making money now and Sam having more success than he'd had in years. Sam kept his head straight, gazing out the windshield. "What are you supposed to do, turn it down?"

"No," I said.

"Anyway," he said, "your dorm room was a mess. I couldn't believe it."

"My roommate," I said.

"Right," said Sam. "You had flags up in there. I don't want you disrespecting the flag."

I was wearing his flack jacket from the Marines and hadn't shaved or cut my hair in weeks, but he didn't say anything about that. "I don't disrespect the flag," I said.

"I fought for that flag."

"Among other things, Dad," I said. "But we're not fighting about those things this time. I'm not dying over there, Sam. I'll die when they come over here."

"I don't want you to die," he said. "I want you to respect the flag."

In a lot of ways it was an argument already old and dry. He and Gil fought it out when Gil quit ROTC at Stuben College. Now Gil had a job with Kodak up in Rochester, New York. He wasn't in the army. And the issue was over for me when Sam let me wear his flack jacket. But we didn't have a lot to talk about anymore and it let us talk about something besides what we all owed Callahan.

So within the week I was back at Dan's, drinking in his parlor while he worked in his office, because if we talked, we fought. After midnight he'd call me upstairs.

One night, early in the summer, he came down and poured himself a drink and sat across from me. "So," he said, "all *B*'s again Mr. Rosenthal."

"I got an *A* in Intro to Philosophy."

"Indeed."

"It interested me, Cal." He let me call him Cal now, like all his old friends.

"What interested you?" he asked.

"Metaphysics."

"You got an *A* in metaphysics?"

"I got an *A* in Intro," I said. "I just wrote a paper, then the term ended."

"We didn't cancel any classes at St. Mary's," Dan Callahan said. He sipped his drink and rubbed his chin. "I'm a little worried about you. Maybe Manfred is a little too liberal and unstructured."

"I like it," I said.

"What do you like?"

"I have friends."

"Like that goof, Mr. Gore," he said. He'd met Rory once and they fought over whether basketball should be fun. Fun, Callahan had said, why that's absurd! Yes, guffawed Rory. Absurd! Yes!

"You looked sluggish this year when you played. Next year you'll have a new coach, you'll have to step up. I won't be there for you. If you played for St. Mary's, you could come here before games."

It was the moment when something snapped. "That'll be okay," I said. "I don't want to do this anymore."

"Do what?" said Dan Callahan.

"I don't want to sleep with you."

"What are you talking about?"

"What we do," I said. "I don't want to do it anymore."

He hesitated, then stared me in the eyes. "I don't know what you're talking about," he said.

"I don't want to have sex anymore. What we do is sex. I don't want to do it."

Callahan sputtered. "You perverted, deluded kid!" he said. "How dare you? You don't know what you're saying."

"I do." I tried to stay calm. "What we do is sex. I really care about you, but I can't take it anymore."

"What can't you take?" demanded Callahan. "Nothing goes on. Nothing happens."

"It disgusts me," I said.

"It disgusts you!" yelled Callahan. "You crazy fucking ass! What are you saying?"

I repeated it. "It disgusts me. I don't care what you call it. It's sex. I don't want to do it anymore."

Callahan's face puffed and blustered. His hands flew in front of him. "If that's what you think, get out of here!" he said. "Get out! Get out of this house! I never want to see you again!"

"All right," I said. "All right. If that's how you feel."

"You're damned right, that's how I feel. You ungrateful bastard. Think of all I've done for you and your family. Think of all I've given you. I made you!"

"Yes," I said softly. "You made me. Thank you. But I'm miserable now."

"Get out!" he yelled. "Get out!"

Instead of going home I walked the streets. I walked for hours, then ended up at a friend's apartment. I poured everything out. He listened quietly.

"You and Callahan?" he finally said.

"I think there are others," I said.

"Wouldn't people know?"

"Who would know?" I said. "Who could say anything?"

I knew he thought I was nuts, making it up. But I went home relieved and slept all day. I'd made the break. I couldn't even think of the consequences. But that night Callahan did something that he'd never before done. He called me.

"Come over," he said. "I'm sorry. I apologize."

I loved him. I saw it as an opportunity for us to move on as friends. And when I arrived that night, it seemed he did, too. He didn't talk about our argument. He made me a drink. "Bourbon, right?" he said. "On the rocks?"

"Yes."

"You're a young adult now," he said to me. He handed me the drink and sat down. "You need to be independent."

"Yes," I said. "Thank you."

"You should have a car."

"Well, I can't afford a car," I said.

"I'll help you get one if you do me a favor."

I hesitated.

"Take a class at St. Mary's. I'll pay for it. It's in ancient Greek philosophy. I just want you to be able to compare us to Manfred. I'll be interested in what you think."

"Okay," I said, "that could be fun."

"I have some connections at City Hall. I'll get you a job with sanitation, working nights so you can go to school and study during the day."

"Garbage collecting."

"Don't scoff. It takes a lot of pull to land those jobs. Only a few kids get them for summer. Senators' kids. Judges'."

"All right," I said.

"Pick out the car and I'll front you the money. Pay me back over the summer."

"Thank you," I said. "That would be great."

"You have to go to City Hall tomorrow. The Mayor's office. They'll expect you."

"Okay."

He paused for a moment. "Let me get you another drink."

"I have to go soon," I said to him.

"No problem, Mr. Rosenthal. Have another drink, then go."

He fixed me another bourbon, then sat down again. "Have you heard anything from Luciani?" he said.

"Raymond?"

"He came to my office the other day. He wanted five thousand dollars."

"For what?"

"He said he had pictures."

"Of what?" I said.

"How should I know?" said Callahan. "But do you know what I told him? I said, 'Let's go, Mr. Luciani. Whatever you've got, come out with it. Whatever you think you have on me, fine, put it out there. If you want to take me on, let's go.'"

"What did he do?" I asked.

"He broke down and cried. He broke down. That crazy kid. Like a baby. Right in my office. I gave him a hundred dollars and sent him home." He laughed hard. "Nobody has anything on me, Mr. Rosenthal. Anybody who wants to take me on should think twice."

Back then I didn't even think once.

The next day I interviewed at City Hall for a garbage collector's job and by Sunday night I was working the garbage trucks. Six nights a week, at two a.m., we met in the truck yard next to the incinerator, then hit our routes. I went into people's backyards with an empty garbage can and stuffed their garbage into mine, then carried it on my shoulder back out to the dump truck. As the new member of the crew, when the back of the truck got full, I went up and stomped down the garbage with my feet. We ran three routes and at the end of each one returned to the incinerator to dump our garbage. The work was hard, but it only took about five or six hours, including dumping and breaks, and when we were done we stopped at a bar in Little Italy and illegally picked up their commercial trash. For that, we got free pizza and beer for breakfast.

Callahan lent me six hundred dollars to buy a 1962 Austin-Healey Sprite convertible, red with two wide white stripes on the hood, leather seats, toggle switches, and sliding, plastic windows. Every morning after work I attended philosophy class, then drove to the river beach where I read Plato and slept in the sun. I loved that car and one weekend I drove to Pittsburgh and picked up Cameron Marney. We drove to a friend of hers summer house in Deep Creek, Maryland to swim and water ski on the reservoir. I was in heaven. On the way back we drank beer and partied with other kids we met on the road. Cameron smoked weed for the first time.

"Did you like it?" I asked her when I kissed her good-bye in front of her home.

"I loved it," she said.

"I love you," I told her.

She lowered her eyes and swayed shyly. That was good enough for me.

Yet at the minimum wage I was taking home little more than one hundred dollars every two weeks, which didn't leave me a lot to spend after I paid Callahan $75 for the car, and though I took a certain working class pride in the calluses on my shoulders and hands, I didn't like working. The good part of the job was the hours. For the first time since I was fourteen I wasn't drinking every night. And I wasn't spending that time with Callahan. And for the first time in years, I wasn't playing basketball. I let my hair grow past my shoulders and cultivated a goatee. I contemplated quitting basketball for good. One weekend when I showed up at Holy Name for a scrimmage, Callahan wouldn't let me play. He ridiculed me in front of everyone for my long hair. He called me a hippie and, ironically, a girl.

In the middle of the summer Manfred's new coach, Jack Crowder, called me up and brought me to a local gym for a workout with Manfred's starting guard from the year before, Tommy Jones. I could usually out-play Tommy Jones and I did that day as well. Crowder was a crew-cut, military type, full of slogans and rough pep. After the workout I told him I was thinking of not coming out for the team.

"Why not?" he said.

"Can you use me?" I said.

"I don't know," he said.

"That's why not," I said.

One Sunday night near the end of August, I went over to Callahan's to drop off the $75 before work. I'd finished my philosophy course. I got a *B+*, recorded as a *B*.

"Professor Lynn said you have a fine mind," said Callahan. "You're just undisciplined. You lack intellectual rigor."

"I deserved an *A*," I said.

"All students think they deserve *A*'s," said Callahan. "They *all* do. But you got a *B*."

There was a point being proved. About St. Mary's. About my *B+* mind. But I'd had it. I'd had enough of everything. I wanted to be something else, somebody else.

But I still owed Callahan $150. Four more weeks of collecting garbage right up till the beginning of school. I'd been drinking and smoking pot that evening and wasn't looking forward to beginning my week of lugging other people's trash. Callahan sensed it.

"You've worked hard this summer," he said. "Why not quit?"

"I still owe you $150," I said.

"You've fulfilled your part of the bargain," said Callahan. "Forget about the last $150."

I hesitated.

"You don't have to leave for work yet," said Dan Callahan. "Get yourself a drink and sit down."

I poured myself a bourbon on the rocks. We talked about Holy Name basketball. They'd won the state title again. I finished my drink and he got me another. After that, he again suggested that I quit collecting garbage.

"It's okay," he said. "Call in. Tell them you're done. Forget about the money."

I went to the phone and called in to work. I told the supervisor that I wasn't coming in that night. I told him that I was done for good. I felt relief. A little guilt. But I got myself another bourbon and sat down in front of Callahan.

"Well," he said. "Great! You did it! Now finish up that drink and get upstairs."

For a $150 I was his boy again.

Twenty-four

⸺◦◦◦◦⸺

Before going back to Manfred I met a girl in Stuben at a party. Her name was Dorthea. She went to Stuben College and was from Albany, New York. She was thin and sallow, brown-eyed, open-hearted. She had some acne scars, but so did I. She was Puerto Rican and part black. We were hippies together. We got stoned, drove around in my little car, went to movies, ate pizza, sat by the river and necked and, finally, made love. It was my first time. I imagined I was Cameron. I got hard. I didn't come. Neither did she. I shook with self-doubt and determination to be normal. Then I left for Manfred.

That fall, Manfred's nationally ranked soccer team refused to get haircuts and quit *en masse*. The football team held together. Crowder let it be known that the basketball team, including the eight black freshman recruits who wore sideburns and Afros, would sport short haircuts. There were only two veterans who didn't live in the athletic team dorm and didn't already have short hair, Rory Gore and me.

For Rory, hair wasn't political, it was irrelevant. When you played basketball you joined up, you said *yes* to Wall Street and the army and all of it, so who gave a fuck if you played with long hair or not. There were bigger reasons not to play, but if he did decide to play basketball he'd just get a haircut.

"It's a symbol," I said.

"It's about your body, not symbols," said Rory Gore.

One of the new freshman, Marvin Wilson, took me aside.

"Crowder said you're seeing a black girl up in Stuben," he said.

"Part," I said. "How does Crowder know?"

"She can't be part black."

"Then talk to Lacy," I said. Lacy was the only black veteran on the team and he dated a white.

"He ain't even part black," said Marvin. "He's an Oreo. In the ROTC."

"What do you want me to change?" I said. "I'm seeing a white girl, too."

"That just makes it worse," said Marvin. "You getting a hair cut? We could all refuse."

"We," I said. Me and Rory and you guys."

"That's right," said Marvin.

"You on one of those academic scholarships?" I said.

"Yes."

"Well?" I said.

"I see," said Marvin Wilson.

In truth, I was much more intense about Cameron Marney than I was about Dorthea, basketball, or the war. I ran around campus looking for her on my first night back, finally finding her perched on a wall listening to a band outside the big cafeteria. She seemed almost disappointed to see me, but eventually warmed up. I raved around her frantically. What should I do about my life? What should I do about basketball? What should I do about my hair?

"Oh, play basketball," she said. "Don't you want to be a basketball star?"

"Do you want me to be a basketball star?"

She did her demure thing, looking down, then tossing her hair. "Sure," she said. "Why not?"

I thought I'd just been talking about why not. But what mattered most was that I wanted a girlfriend. I needed a girlfriend more than anything. It didn't matter if I had to masturbate twice a day. So on October 1st I attended the first of the unofficial practices, half-court and full-court scrimmages, watched by Crowder's assistants, that you didn't have to attend unless you wanted to make the team. Rory came, too. Official practices started on November 1. Haircuts were due on October 30. On November 15 we'd play our first exhibition against the Columbus AAU.

Practices were hell. Crowder was a strict disciplinarian. We ran lengthy conditioning drills, sometimes going for hours without ever touching a basketball. But as much as I disliked him, with his silly, rough-pep slogans that we had to memorize before every practice and his long speeches about self-sacrifice, everything had changed. He taught me a ton about ball handling and defense. As a team we were hungry, disciplined, and confident.

So on October 30th I cut my hair and shaved and so did Rory Gore. I ran to Cameron, of course, who eyed me skeptically.

"You look so different," she said.

"Of course I do," I said.

"You were so tan and handsome with your long hair."

"You told me you wanted me to play basketball," I said.

"I know," she cooed. "I told you. Isn't that the problem?"

"What problem?" I said. "What's love got to do with haircuts?"

She lowered her head. She frowned. Two weeks later I found out I was starting against the Columbus AAU and that afternoon before the game Cameron Marney dumped me.

I wept in front of her. I begged her to reconsider. She cried, too.

"Chuck, this will never work."

"It was working," I said.

"You're younger than me, and crazy. You're very intense."

"Yes?"

"I'm Presbyterian," she said. "A WASP."

"I'm hardly Jewish at all," I said.

She shook her head.

"I'm wide open on the God thing."

She couldn't look at me. She turned and walked away.

I arrived for the scrimmage in a rage.

"Whoa, my friend," said Rory Gore.

"Cameron left me. I'm going to kill somebody," I said. I didn't kill anybody. I scored forty points and held their leading scorer to four. Afterward he told Crowder he'd never faced anybody like me. Well, I'd never faced anybody like me either. I came into the season like a maniac. After our next exhibition against Division II Central State, their coach took me aside and asked if I was interested in a scholarship. "Believe me," I told him, "I have one."

We swept our first four independent games, then played our last game before Christmas break against Rochester, the defending league co-champions. For the first time in memory, our gym was packed. We had our first winning record in twenty years. When we came out for warm-ups, the place shook. I looked across the way before starting line-ups were introduced and there, in the

bleachers across from our bench, sat Cameron. When I was intro-
duced, in the darkened gym under a spotlight, I ran out screaming
at the top of my lungs with my fist in the air. The crowd roared.
The lights came on. Rory went to the center for the jump ball.
Rochester's all-conference guard sidled up next to me and said,
"What the fuck's with you guys?"

He found out. Last year they'd beaten us by thirty in their
gym, twenty in ours. This time they were up by only two at half.
In the second half they pulled away and then we fought back.
When I hit a reverse lay-up with thirty seconds left, we finally
caught them. They called time out to set up the last shot. But
Crowder had shown us film after film on Rochester. We let them
come down the floor and work the clock down to ten seconds,
then they set up a backdoor. Their point guard hit the post and
my man took off behind me for the basket. I was ready. I peeled
back and picked off the pass, headed down the floor and sank a
shot above the key with no time left. The crowd came out of the
stands and mobbed us.

I got headlines in the Manfred and Stuben sports pages. My
parents called, and I called Callahan who said, "Congratulations,
Mr. Rosenthal. You did it. You're a star. Now aren't you glad you
didn't quit over hair?"

Hair-shmair. After practice I ran to Cameron Marney's dorm
and stood in front of her breathless when she opened her door.

She stuttered. "Chuck," she said. "Congratulations."

I put my hand out to touch her cheek and she stepped back.
"I'm glad you came by," she said. She went into her room and came
out with a brown paper sack. "This is your stuff," she said.

"I don't want it."

She dropped it in front of me. She left it there. And I left it
there. If I was mad before, now I was madder than ever. I thought
I was mad at her.

Rory and I had never stopped dropping acid, smoking pot, and
getting drunk, not even now, well into the season, but that night I
hung one on good, like the night in Nassau. I wandered to a campus dance and sat in the corner on the floor, staring out at the
bodies and lights; all that great, long hair, people in love and dancing and not giving a shit about basketball stars. Bob Angel found
me there. He was with his sometimes girl friend, Collette, and he

took me by the hand to his room where they both made love to me. And I made love to both of them; my first anal sex, as the recipient, with Angel. I came with a woman for the first time with Collette.

"Aah Rosenthal, Rosenthal," Angel said. "Who would have thought?"

"You're going to be all right, Rosenthal," said Collette. "You're way too much for that sorority chick. You're going to grow up and be a good lover."

"Grow up?" I said.

"You're going to have lots of girls," Collette said to me. "Lots of girls."

If Collette was open to sleeping with anybody she liked, I respected her for it. And the Angel, though he didn't describe himself as bisexual, he loved women and liked sex. He never made love to men alone, but he never let a man being involved get in the way of his making love to a woman. He wasn't very good looking; squat, his face a bit pock-marked, but outside of Rory he was the most seductive individual I've ever known.

That night, if I thanked Callahan for making me a basketball star, I thanked him, as well, for making me capable of performing the sex I had that night, a sexuality I was certain he'd abhor.

Rory and Anna pitched in, too. A few days later, they bitched and joked that I'd made love to Angel and Collette and not them.

"What's wrong with us?" said Anna.

"Ask Lola," I said to her.

"Fuck Lola," Anna said.

"I wish I had," I said.

They sat down on either side of me and began caressing my hair and ears. They pressed me between them. They made love to me, though Rory operated more as a facilitator as we took turns with Anna. We dropped acid and roamed the campus, then the streets of Manfred, marveling at the play of streetlight in the frozen, cement sidewalks, tracing with our fingertips the bark of trees. I felt like a kid with a half-dozen lives, each hidden from the other.

I was an enigma to me and more of an enigma to Crowder, who turned out to be as militaristic as they came, but he couldn't deny my intensity. During one practice, while he was advocating a pressing man-to-man, saying that nobody could dribble up court against a press and then have the energy to hit a long jump shot with a hand in his face, he asked the team who the best shooter was. Several people pointed to me. He put a man on me and I worked up the court and hit a fade-away from the top of the key. When I did it again Crowder himself guarded me the third time. I hit it against him, too. The fourth time, against Crowder again, I missed. "See?" said Crowder, and everybody laughed, even Crowder.

Often, I stayed after practice to work on my shooting, my defense, and my passing. At night, I drank, I smoked pot, opium, even PCP. I tripped on LSD with Rory Gore. Somehow or another, I was taking it all out on somebody. I thought it was Cameron Marney.

"No!" said Rory Gore. "It's something much, much deeper. But it's making you the craziest, best basketball player in the world!"

That Christmas break I returned to Stuben a hero. At Callahan's request I came by Holy Name and scrimmaged with his varsity which was headed for another state championship. The kids gathered around me worshipfully, full of questions.

"Why isn't your name on a State Title banner?"

"We didn't win the city," I said. "We were the worst team in Holy Name history."

"That one?" they said, pointing to the record board where our season stood at 18–11.

"Yes."

"He was horrible. The whole team was horrible," said Dan Callahan.

"You weren't MVP?" someone asked.

"Not here," I said. "Not even in high school."

"So you see gentlemen," Callahan exclaimed. "There's hope! With hard work, there's hope for all of you."

Especially, I hoped, for Joe, who in seventh grade was still under five feet tall. Like Gil he was going to grow late. He wasn't big enough to compete and other kids with less skill could now out-muscle him. He didn't have the disposition to fight back. Joe was fair, almost blond, with huge, blue eyes and delicate skin. His beauty was almost effeminate, almost angelic. When I met his eyes that day he stared at me with a kind of anguish that I met with disdain. I couldn't imagine, that with that look, he was wondering what I had to go through with Callahan; if the unimaginable thing that he was doing was something I did, too. And how could I know that? Who could?

That night I dropped by on Dan. He was Academic Vice-President now and had a new, bigger house closer to St. Mary's. He wasn't downstairs and I let myself in by his unlocked back door. I poured myself a drink and sat down, then heard some noise coming from the stairs. A boy appeared. He looked about fourteen. He was slender, dressed in khakis and a sweater, but freshly scrubbed, as if he'd just come out of the shower. He looked at me demurely, almost shamefully. Then Callahan came down the stairs.

"Mr. Rosenthal," he said. "I'll be right back. Make yourself welcome while I take this young man home."

I couldn't face it. I could neither face it nor admit it. I went to the cupboard, grabbed a bottle of Jack Daniels and left.

Back at Manfred we roared through January, going undefeated in league play and heading for our showdown with undefeated Carnegie in Pittsburgh. Carnegie Tech was a school four times our size that had won or shared the conference title for five years running. For the first time in Manfred's history travel busses had been rented to caravan our fans to an away game and our cheerleaders were going to travel with the team.

The night before the big game Rory and I walked out of practice and into the cold, Ohio night, those dreadful stars which spawned astronomy twinkling above us, the narrow sidewalk gray and dry between mounds of piled snow.

"Do you think we'll win, my friend?" Rory asked me.

"Yes."

"Because we have you," he said.

"Because everything's different. I hate Crowder, but we're good now."

"But how do we deal with all this pressure?" said Rory, unfolding a sheet of windowpane LSD.

It was really good acid and we took too much of it. We tripped our brains out. We piled into Rory's '53 Chevy and rolled into the night, finally stopping in the woods where we wandered, waxed inanely, walked and walked among the bare trees until dawn and we were still tripping.

"What to do?" I said.

"The game is far away," said Rory Gore.

"What do you think will happen?" I said. "We can't really take queludes and get drunk."

"We'll come down eventually, my friend."

So I arrived with Rory at the bus in the early afternoon, haggard and giddy, things still moving at the edge of my vision.

Crowder eyed us suspiciously. "You boys all right?" he said.

"Just a little anxious, Coach," I told him.

On the bus we had to sit by ourselves so we wouldn't talk. We were supposed to be thinking about the game. That's the way it always was. If we won we could talk on the way home. This time we had the added madness of the cheerleading squad chattering away in the seats in front of us. I had a crush on the captain, Sandra Horowitz. Every heterosexual male on campus had a crush on Sandra Horowitz; thick, straight auburn hair, brown eyes and freckles, full lips. Her body was round where it should be round and tight everywhere else. She'd just broken up with the tailback of the football team, a blond hunk of a guy who looked like Adonis. I knew, because everybody knew. Socially and physically, people knew her every move.

Crowder'd been explicit about the cheerleaders. No talking to the cheerleaders on the bus. I listened to the blend of their voices, the stream of their giggling, their conversation like a song and like wind. I let their voices rock me with the bus drone. I looked over at Rory who stared out the window, his tongue hanging like a dog. I tried to sleep, but I couldn't. I was worried.

When we hit Carnegie Rory pulled me aside. "I give up," he said. "Let's get stoned."

"No," I said. "No." I went to a toilet stall, my stomach flipping, my mind still goosey from the acid. Well, what if I played poorly? What if we lost? I took a hot shower, then a cold one, rubbed myself with a scratchy towel, then put my clothes back on and wandered out to watch the freshman game. There was a time-out and as our fans arrived, filing in off the busses to fill the half-empty gym, I walked along the sideline, looking for Rory. I sat down. The cheerleaders danced in the middle of the floor, trying to get our fans to start chanting as they came in off the bus, then the game resumed and they rushed to the sideline where I sat.

"Hey, Chuck Rosenthal, you going to win?" said Sandy Horowitz.

I held my head.

"You okay?"

"Nervous," I said.

"I wish I could play," said Sandy. "I really wish I could play them."

"I wish you could, too," I said and we laughed.

It seemed like out of nowhere, but now Crowder was standing in front of me.

"Where's Gore?" he said.

"I don't know."

"What are you doing here with the cheerleaders?"

"They came to me," I said.

"You knew where they were sitting. I said no talking to the cheerleaders."

"On the bus," I said.

Crowder's jaw tightened. "You're suspended," he said.

"Suspended?"

"Indefinitely. Don't dress." He walked away.

"Jesus," said Sandy.

"I guess I don't have to move now," I said.

But the game ended a few minutes later anyway. I went down to the locker room with the team, where Crowder explained I wouldn't be playing because I broke team rules. He readjusted his game plan and sent them out to warm up. The place was packed and buzzing. People started to chant back and forth at each other and cheer. This was the big game and despite everything I wanted to be in it.

During shoot around, Rory came over to the end of the bench.

"What did you do?" he said.

"I talked to a cheerleader."

"My friend!" laughed Gore, snapping his finger in front of him emphatically. "You are so smart!"

"I didn't plan it," I said. "It just happened."

"Yes! It just happened!" said Rory Gore. "Now watch me!"

I did. Rory played like a man possessed by the Void. The ball bounced off his wrists. His shots floated weightlessly. After ten minutes, down by fifteen, Crowder pulled him. Crowder stormed down to the end of the bench. "What's he on?" he raged at me.

I raised my eyes to him. "Nothing," I said to Crowder. "Too much nothing."

Crowder studied my eyes, but I imagine, by now, they were just filled with the lights of the auditorium.

"I do not understand your generation," Crowder said to me.

"Let me play, Coach," I said.

Five minutes later, down by twenty-two, the Carnegie fans singing and laughing in the stands, Crowder walked down to the end of the bench again. "Suspension's over," he said. "Get dressed. Hurry. I'll call a couple time outs."

I dressed in absolute calm. The pounding and cheering in the gym above me sounded like a chant, calling me above. Back on the bench, next to Crowder, the place felt huge and warm. I looked up into the stands and I liked everybody. All of them. I could see everything and everyone in absolute detail and the game unfolded in front of me as if in slow motion. There were two minutes left in the half. "Get in there," Crowder said.

Suddenly, I never felt better in my life. It was as if there was no separation between my hands, the ball, and the rim. Four times we came down the floor. Four times I shot and scored. At half we were down by twenty.

Crowder told us to hang in there. They'd come back to us and that's when we'd make our run. When we went back on the floor, our fans clapped listlessly and Carnegie's laughed and booed. I turned and pointed at them. They yowled back.

"Stop that," Crowder yelled at me.

Rory, who wasn't getting back in, laughed.

Crowder was a good preparation coach, but not a good game coach. I remembered an old Callahan-ism, that teams that made comebacks usually let up at the moment they caught the other team, especially away from home. I walked over to Crowder. "We're going to catch them, Coach," I said. "When we catch them, call time out and remind everybody the game is just starting."

I scored the first ten points of the half. If before everything was in slow motion, now it was all silence and fury. The basket was an ocean. We cut the lead to ten in the first few minutes. They called time out and settled down, but we surged again with five minutes to go and cut it to four. They called time out again. "Don't let up!" I yelled like a madman in our huddle. "Don't let up!" With two minutes to go, we caught them.

Crowder called time. He didn't know what to say. As we stood there sweating, now I could hear the pounding and roaring from the bleachers. I met Crowder's eyes. There, across a generation and a hundred differences, at that little big game between a couple of nobody schools, whoever he was, and me within my many selves, our eyes met and we both wanted to win.

"Let's go to a zone, just to throw them off, Coach," I said. "Two times down, then we can go back to the man-to-man."

"All right," said Crowder. "Two-three zone, twice down."

"Don't let up," I said quietly.

"It's a brand new game," said Crowder. "Gather yourselves. Start now. Don't let up."

Carnegie wasn't ready for the zone. They threw the ball right into my hands and I hit a left-hand running drive. They missed the next time down. I hit from outside. They threw the ball away again when we went back to the man-to-man and they had to start fouling. The game was over. Little Manfred College, which hadn't had a winning season in twenty years, was in first place. I scored thirty-seven, had eight rebounds, four steals and six assists; the best game of my life. I was a basketball star. I wanted it all then. I wanted everything Callahan said I should have, everything he said I would want.

When we came out of the locker room our fans were all over us. All around us plans for victory parties were being made. No practice tomorrow. The parties would start as soon as we all got home.

Rory put his arm around me. "Holy shit," he said. "You're going to hate this."

But when I walked onto the bus I stood between the rows of cheerleaders and put out my hands. I said, "Who wants to go to a party?"

"Me," Sandy Horowitz said.

Chapter Twenty-five

⊸⊸⊸⊸

It was January, 1971. There was a fine line between hippie and cheerleader, football player and freak. Sandy and I got stoned and dropped a quarter hit each of window pane. We hopped from frat house to frat house, from one victory party to the next. Everywhere people gave us drinks and beer. They cheered us. They asked me to join their fraternities. The basketball star and the captain of the cheerleaders.

We walked to my little room just a block off campus, where I had a writing desk, a radio, and a single mattress on the floor. For the first time in my life I had sex without imagining I was a girl. In the morning we made love again.

"You hugged me all night," Sandy said to me. "You're a hugger."

"Maybe I am."

"You have really soft skin."

"Want to go to Niagara Falls?" I said.

"How long?"

"Four of five hours. It'll take a day."

"Okay," said Sandy Horowitz. "Let's go."

We jumped in the Sprite and headed for Canada, top down, heat on full blast. We talked and kissed and clung. We got to the Falls in time for the last icy ride on The Maid of the Mist, strolled along the Canadian side as the night fell, the multi-colored spotlights dancing over the amazing waterfalls. We stopped and gazed at the water. Sandy grabbed me around the neck and gave me a huge kiss.

"Let's not get serious, okay?" she said.

"This looks pretty serious to me."

"Do you think people are talking?"

"About us?"

"Yes."

"Do you want them to be talking?"

"Yes."

"Let's go," I said.

We dropped some speed and drove back to Manfred where, swept up in my celebrity status, I knocked on the door of a frat house and asked for a bottle of wine. A few brothers came out.

"Where you two been?"

"Niagara Falls."

"No shit!"

They came through with two bottles and a basket of bread and cheese. We ate and drank in my room, then around one in the morning smoked a joint.

"Want to go swimming?" I asked her.

"How?"

"Come on," I said.

We bundled up and walked to the old pool where I hopped through the window then ran around and opened the door for Sandy. Alone in the warm basement pool, lit only by an exit sign over the door, we swam together in the nude, wet, touching each other, exploring, hugging. The old locker room had ancient showers with wide, flat shower heads that extended down from the ceiling about seven feet high. Even Rory could stand under them. The hot water fell in a thick circle of fat streams. We soaped and washed each other. We made love standing up. She was a beautiful girl. And I was a beautiful boy. It was the hardest I'd ever been in my life.

Those next two weeks were the halcyon days. We won four more times. When we played at home or close to Manfred, Sam and Helen drove to the games, bringing Joe and Andy along, and sometimes even Sylvie. In Rochester, where we won again, Gil showed up and asked Crowder if he could take me out for a hamburger and drive me back to Manfred on his way to Stuben. Sandy slipped out on the cheerleaders and Gil took us out for burgers and beer. That night, we slept on an air mattress in the living room floor of his apartment.

Sandy and I made love everyday. We walked through campus arm in arm, hip to hip. As she liked to say, "Are we an item or what?"

Though teams began to put their best defensive player on me, it didn't matter much. I simply put them to sleep in the first five minutes by running around like a maniac and not shooting. Once lulled, I popped them, and their confidence shattered. Rory didn't start anymore and I saw less of him because of the time I spent with Sandy, but we got together a couple times. Once we tripped, and once, over at his house where he lived with a couple of railroad men, we made chocolate chip cookies and stayed up all night eating warm cookies and drinking milk. We seldom talked about the team, but one time that night he turned to me, shook his fist, and said, "I should crush that Crowder like a bug." Then he laughed. "Ah-ha!"

I talked with Callahan sometimes. I began to see him as a man with the utmost ability to understand others and almost no ability to understand himself. This made him manipulative. And it was why he didn't know that he loved me or that my therapy was sex. Yet on the brink of quitting only a few months ago, I now possessed everything he said I would achieve. I was a star. I had a girl. If my fantasy life was still confused, well, I now had little time for it. What I did in bed with him seemed far away and a small price to have paid for it all. As he said, he'd made me. I thanked him.

"No need to thank me," said Dan Callahan. "It was your hard work. You take the credit for yourself, Mr. Rosenthal."

"I couldn't have done it without you," I said.

"You'll be the highest scorer in the history of Manfred College. All-Conference, maybe even an honorable mention All-American if you go to the NCAA's."

And now there was talk of it. Even Crowder talked about it. If we took the conference we could get a bid. If we kept winning, we might get ranked in the Top Twenty. Up next, we had an away game at last place Wheelton College in West Virginia. Wheelton was so bad that they were one of the teams we'd beaten last year. Crowder warned us. Wheelton could be tough at home. They were an upset trap. But it was impossible not to be over-confident. After our four hour bus ride into the West Virginia hills, the Wheelton cafeteria seemed to have no knowledge that we were supposed to be fed. Our locker room wasn't heated. When we hit the floor, the place was packed with hissing hokies. The refs were teachers from local high schools.

They came out in a box-and-one on me. They held us, scratched us, clobbered us. Crowder screamed and got a technical. With two people on me everywhere I went, I convinced Crowder to let me move into the post, the middle of the offense, which basically transformed their box-and-one into a two-one-two zone, but when I dished off to our second and third scorers they missed from the outside. We went in at half time down by some ridiculous score like 30–20.

Crowder raged about everything in the locker room, our poor treatment, the referees, our poor rebounding, our lousy shooting; how he'd warned us this would happen. When he was done, he stood in front of us as we sat there shivering in our warm-ups.

After a little while I said, "So Coach, what do you want to do?"

"You guys have to pick it up," he said.

"If you want me to get more shots, Coach, let's just run our man-to-man offense." It's what Callahan would do. He confused and shattered all specialty zones—match-ups, box-and-ones, triangle-and-twos—simply by running man-to-man. "And let someone besides me bring the ball up."

For all our differences, this is where Crowder and I met. "Okay," he said. "Let's try that."

It worked. In ten minutes we'd tied the game. After Wheelton called time-out, then came down the floor and missed, I raced down the court on a fast break. Two men took me out, one over and one under. In the pile-up, somebody put a finger in my right eye. I felt the blood race down my cheek and reached up to find my eyeball slightly dislodged. I panicked. I don't think I screamed. I held my eye. There was some cheering, I think, but soon a doctor was over me. He calmed me down and popped my eye back in. But it was bruised and scratched. I was out of the game and we lost.

Crowder personally took me to a specialist who thought the eye might heal on its own. But it might not. If not, I'd need surgery. In any case, I was going to be out for a long time, maybe for the rest of the year.

Chapter Twenty-six

In the next two weeks we dropped three games, one in the league and two independents. I sat on the end of the bench in my blue Manfred blazer, wearing an eye patch. I watched practices from the bleachers. The losses made Crowder irritable at practice as he tried to fill the scoring gap. He yelled more, particularly at Rory, who responded with more incompetence and irrelevance the more intense Crowder became.

"What is the matter with you?" Crowder yelled, stopping practice to single him out. "Are you on drugs?"

Rory calmly lowered his hands to his sides and opened his palms. "It's the Inverse Square Law," said Rory Gore.

"What are you talking about?"

"The Inverse Square Law of Ridicule," Rory said.

"You are going to run after practice, Mr. Gore," said Crowder. "You are going to run your ass off."

Rory shrugged. "Did you know there was a war going on?" he said. He turned to everybody. "I think what we're doing here is saying *yes* to the war by ignoring it. Do we want to say *yes* to the war?"

"You'd be fighting in that war without this, Mr. Gore," said Crowder.

"Okay," said Rory. "I quit. I quit." He spread his long arms to the whole team. "And I'm not just quitting over Vietnam," he announced. "I'm doing it for all the dead people everywhere. All of them." He walked off the floor.

"That boy is crazy," Crowder said to me.

"Buddha don't play basketball," I said.

"Buddha what?" said Crowder.

Rory Gore had stopped playing organized basketball for good. I laughed with him about it, but I'd changed and he knew it.

"You're a fucking star," he said. He wagged his head and stuck out his tongue. "You're a fucking silly basketball star."

He was right. Before and after practice I worked the floor, trying to train myself, without depth perception, to spot.shoot from designated places on the court. But my peripheral vision was nonexistent and in pick-up games, when bodies flew by me, I shied.

"Stop playing," Crowder finally yelled at me. "Get off the floor before you hurt yourself worse."

But suddenly, under the pressure, his great renaissance going up in smoke, everything about me bugged him, as if it weren't my injury that set the team back, but me. That night after chasing me off the floor he called me into his office.

"I was hurt once, Rosenthal," he said. "I was on my way to our biggest game of the season and I saved a little girl who wandered into the street in front of a speeding car. I had to dive to save her. I got hurt, too. I felt horrible, but I played that night. I didn't find out until after that I'd played the whole game on a broken leg."

"That's amazing, Coach," I said.

"Not to blow my own horn," said Crowder.

"Not at all, Coach," I said, "But you told me to get off the floor."

"And you listened," he said. "That's part of the problem."

"Listening," I said.

"You have to know when to listen," Crowder said to me. "And you talk too much. I don't want you giving advice in the huddle anymore."

"That's not leadership?"

"No. It's disrespect."

"What was Rory's problem?" I said to him.

"I didn't think I could say this until now, Rosenthal," he said, "but I think you're a disruptive influence to the team. Dating cheerleaders. Your living off campus instead of in the athlete dorm. And I worry about your lifestyle. You and Gore." He looked away, then down. He looked me in the eyes. "I know about marijuana," he said.

"Coach," I said, "the team is everything to me. I'd do anything to play."

"Look at your hair," he said.

It was true. My hair was growing out and I'd started a mustache, but what could he do, not play me? Finally he came out with it. He didn't want me traveling with the team for away games. Particularly because of Sandy, I was a distraction.

"What do you think of that?" I said to Sandy that night.

It didn't matter that much to her, she said, because she wanted to stop seeing me. A week later she was dating the star shortstop of the baseball team. Getting the jump on spring. It broke my heart. How could all this happen so fast?

The next away game, I stayed home and got stoned with Rory Gore. "Think about it," said Rory. "Life could be like this."

"I'm trying to figure out if it will be my fault for listening to Crowder and staying home," I said.

"My friend," said Rory Gore. "More wine!"

Manfred lost, but won the next home game. There was one game left, at home against Carnegie Tech, now only one game back in the standings. I sat at the end of the bench. I watched Sandy cheer. I watched Manfred lose. Our national ranking was kaput. Our NCAA bid long gone.

There was no play-off format in our conference, long a gentlemen's conference that accepted ties, and Carnegie Tech appealed to us to accept the traditional co-championship. Crowder wanted to force a play-off and called us in for a team meeting to vote on it.

"We'll show them this time," he said.

"Coach," I said, "we're co-champions. Our first winning season since before most of us were born. Let's take it."

By show of hands, the team voted to play and I was the only dissenting vote.

"You mean this isn't unanimous?" Crowder said to the air.

"Oh, you meant *play* them for the title," I said, raising my hand.

After that I got called in again. Crowder sat behind his desk, his office covered with blue and gold banners, slogans like, "A winner never quits. A quitter never wins." He had pictures of his high school state title teams on the walls. "Rosenthal," he said, not looking me in the eyes but fumbling with a pencil in front of him, "I mean this as no offense to you as a person, or to your play and to what you've contributed to the team, but your aberrant lifestyle has made me reconsider nominating you for All-Conference."

"I led the league in scoring," I said to him.

"Only for half the season."

"Two-thirds," I said.

"Next year I want a good haircut. I want you living in the team dorm. No Rory Gore. No drugs."

"Coach, it's my personal life. I played hard for you."

"I'm telling you, Rosenthal," he said. "I'm not doing this out of vindictiveness. I'm doing this to motivate you."

I stood. "Coach," I said to him, "you got it all wrong."

Wrong or right, Carnegie Tech slaughtered us. Manfred's greatest season in twenty years ended.

"Who the fuck cares?" Rory said to me that night.

"I do," I said. "At least I think I do."

"Ah-ha! My friend!" said Rory Gore. "Less thought! More wine!"

Chapter Twenty-seven

When I called Callahan about the All-Conference thing he said, "Forget about it. You were hurt. You were an easy target, you couldn't play anyway. He made and example of you now, but next October he'll need you again."

"I don't want that kind of relationship with my coach," I said.

"You had a great year. He can't win without you. Why don't you celebrate and join me and Wooj in Nassau again?"

"I made plans to drive to Florida with Gil," I said.

"Florida? With all those yahoos?"

"There were plenty of them in Nassau," I said.

"Suit yourself, Mr. Rosenthal," said Dan Callahan. "Suit yourself."

I hitched up to Rochester, then Gil and I drove his '69 Roadrunner down Route 1. That car was so hot that it shook when it idled. "Gallons per mile," said Gil. We only stopped for gas. South of D.C., into the Carolinas, flowers bloomed and in Georgia the new green grass broke bright against the red clay dirt. We pulled into hot Fort Lauderdale and rented a hotel room with eight other guys. We got drunk and sat around the pool. We only went to the beach once. "I'm here for the booze and sun, not the culture," said Gil. Me, too. We stayed a week, then took the I-75 back, looping west through the green, cold hills of Tennessee and through the horse country of Kentucky where the grass wasn't really blue. Then Gil dropped me off at Manfred. I had a great time.

That year in the north it snowed through April and into the beginning of May. In May, it rained. Then spring broke suddenly and gloriously onto southern Ohio. There was some property the college owned on a stream in the middle of the woods about ten miles out of town and a lot of freaks met out there to drink wine, smoke pot, jump off a little bridge into the run-off swollen stream and run shivering to a nearby meadow to lie naked in the sun. The late spring days rolled long and slow. I met a painter, a writhe, black-haired girl named Sonya Pulski who made love to me in a sunny patch in the woods above the bridge before she even knew who I was.

"You're Chuck Rosenthal?" she said. "Holy shit, I fucked an asshole."

"First time, I bet."

"Is that some kind of locker room humor?"

"Do you want to do it again?"

"That's why it's so big," she said. "You're black."

"I'm not black."

"All basketball players are black," said Sonya Pulski.

"Want to go for a ride in my car?"

"My first jock," Sonya Pulski said.

"A lot of firsts," I said. "How come you know so much about me?"

She came over and sat on my lap, wrapping her legs around my waist. "Oooooh," said Sandra Pulski. She grabbed my hair in both of her fists. "Oooooh."

Twenty-eight

The Sprite died that spring. The engine blew up. The bottom fell out. My eye healed. As soon as Manfred let out in June, I hitchhiked to Toledo, Rory's hometown, where he'd taken a job on the railroad. He expected to flunk the draft physical for being too big.

Flaming Joe from just outside Pittsburgh was visiting, too, with two gay friends. He made Groucho Marx eyebrows at me. "Why do you think they call me Flaming Joe?" he said.

"It ain't because of the Egyptian cupcakes?" I said.

"Are you afraid?" said Flaming Joe.

"I'm not afraid," I said.

Rory had work the first night and Flaming Joe, along with Alex and James, his two friends who both lived in Toledo, wanted to go to a transvestite burlesque dressed in drag.

"Are you afraid now?" said Flaming Joe.

"Yes," I said. "Now I'm a little afraid."

"Have you ever dressed in drag?" said James.

"I thought *you* were dressing in drag," I said. "Not me."

"Come on now," said Alex. "Look at him."

"Look at me what?" I said.

"You've got great hair. You wouldn't even need a wig," said Flaming Joe.

"I've worn my mother's clothes," I said. "Just not in public."

"Make up?" said James.

"Barely," I said.

"Ever slept with a man?" said Alex.

"Guess," I said.

"No," Alex said. "I mean, no, you haven't."

"Twice," said James.

"You missed by about 998," I said.

"Rosenthal," said Flaming Joe. "Rosenthal. Rosenthal. Rosenthal."

"I'm kind of big," I said. "You got big enough stuff."

"Oh, we've got big enough stuff," said James.

I was far from home. Nobody knew me. And I wasn't going out trying to pass as a girl, I'd be with other guys, in drag in a gay club. We drove to Alex and James'. Flaming Joe made martini's and we passed joints. I snorted my first cocaine, which didn't do much, but the amyl poppers made my heart race. James motioned for me to follow him, then stopped outside the bathroom and handed me a razor.

"Shave?" I said.

"Now we don't want to do this half-ass, do we? We want to do this right," he said.

I took the razor.

"And when you're done, use the moisturizing lotion," he said. He held out paisley panties and a padded bra with two foam cups to tape to my chest. "We don't want you coming out naked," he said. "There's a robe, too."

I shaved my face, underarms, chest and legs. The shaving made me feel strangely vulnerable. I got hard and waited to calm down before entering the fray again. Despite his name, Flaming Joe didn't flame nearly as much as Alex and James, which was comforting because I needed someone else there who wasn't acting more female than women. We dressed each other. I needed the gin. I wore hose, and a tight, black dress that showed my collar bone, arms, and muscle-bound calves. "Got to show that tight bod," Alex said. Alex and James wore high heels, but Joe said those would kill me. He got me some pumps. They spent a lot of time on my hair and make-up. Nails. "Try to keep it subtle," I said, because A&J were wearing it by the pound. Then we went out. Joe drove. "Four fags in drag in a car," said Flaming Joe.

"Is this how you envisioned it?" said James.

"I never really envisioned it," I said.

"The good part is," said Alex, "that you don't have to be a woman."

"Is that the good part?" I said.

"That's right," said Flaming Joe. "Who knows?"

We paraded into the burlesque, four among many. It wasn't a big stage thing like Callahan had taken me and Wooj to on Paradise Island in Nassau, with a hundred over-dressed, half-nude women. There was a small stage with a couple mikes. Most the acts weren't sexy, but comic impersonations of women like Dolly Parton and Marilyn Monroe. We sat at a table, drinking gin and popping amyl, then the review ended, the juke box came on and guys started dancing. A&J danced together. Flaming Joe looked at me and I shook my head, no. Then a man came over and sat down across from me and Joe.

He was a big guy, bigger than me. A black man. He had broad shoulders. He wore a pale shirt open at the collar, leather sneakers, tight blue jeans, a Cincinnati Reds baseball cap that he took off and placed in front of him. He was clean shaven and had an Afro that scuffed at his ears.

"Drinks?" he said.

"Sure," said Joe.

The guy put his hand up. The waiter knew what everybody was drinking. I was scared, but I figured whatever happened, I could just say no. Then I thought he was probably interested in Joe and I felt disappointed.

"Raymond," the man said, putting out his hand. "Ray."

Joe shook it. "Josie," he said.

I said, "Chuck."

Joe nodded at me. "First time in drag," he said.

Ray offered a wry smile. "First time for everything," he said.

Mostly he wanted to talk about baseball. I told him I didn't like the Reds.

"Who then?" he said.

"Indians."

"At least they're in Ohio."

A&J came fluttering over and shook his hand. They pulled Joe from his seat and Ray looked at me. "You want to dance?" he said.

"I can't follow," I said.

"Slow one."

"And these shoes."

"Take them off."

"One more drink," I said.

I slugged it down and then went to the crowded dance floor with Ray. Something slow was playing, Streisand, of course. I didn't keep track of her stuff. Ray pulled me to him. He was a big guy and without the heels I could put my head on his shoulder while we danced.

"Athletes body," he said in my ear.

"Uh-huh."

"Track?"

"Basketball," I said.

"Sweet," said Ray.

The song ended. I stepped back. On came Judy Garland and Ray pulled a small, brown bottle from his pocket. It was about the size of his thumb. He unscrewed the lid of the bottle and offered it to me.

"Just pass it under your nose," he said.

I took a big whiff. My mind exploded. Suddenly I was tripping out. The room folded. My knees buckled and Ray caught me, held me, and kissed me. I hardened. He brought me to him and we danced with his hands on my butt. My tits and dick hard, I felt like I'd explode. The dance ended. He took my jaw in his hand and we kissed again.

"You're not supposed to inhale that stuff," he said.

"Just give me more of it."

"Can we go to my place?"

"All right."

I don't know Toledo, but we stayed downtown. He lived near the top of a high-rise from where you could see the lights of the city stretch to the black body of the lake. He made drinks and we danced to jazz. We snorted butyl again, once, twice. I unbuttoned his shirt.

"How do you like it?" said Ray. "Rough? Gentle?"

"I don't really know," I said.

In his bedroom he had a waterbed. He undressed me and we made love, front to front, like with Callahan, first him on top, then me. Before I fell asleep he brought me a huge glass of water and four pills. "You better pre-medicate," he said, "or you're going to feel pretty lousy in the morning." I didn't tell him that I didn't get hangovers. I wasn't turning anything down. I took the pills and slept like a fucking log.

When I woke up he was looking at me. He ran his hand through my hair. Down my arm, across my chest. "You kind of have a body like a black kid," he said. "Stomach and butt, not hair or skin."

"You never know," I said.

"First time in drag, but not first time," he said to me.

"I've had a lover for almost seven years," I said.

"Man?"

"Yes."

"That's a long time. How old are you?"

"Nineteen."

"You were twelve?"

"Thirteen. He doesn't admit we're having sex."

"One of those types," he said.

"That's a type?"

"Yeah," he said. "Unfortunately." He'd stopped stroking me and I touched his cheek, my red nails against his brown flesh.

"I have a girlfriend, too," I said.

"I bet."

"The man was my coach."

Ray sat up and crossed his legs next to me. "That's really young," he said.

"How young is too young?"

"Eighteen is legal."

"Is what we did last night legal?" I said to him. "What if I was eighteen? What if I was seventeen?"

"That's not thirteen," he said.

I sat up now, too. "I chose it," I said, touching his knees. "Like last night. Like now."

Ray studied me. "Some people might say that," he said. "Some might call it pederasty."

"Like the Greeks."

"This isn't Ancient Greece. Some people might call it child molestation," said Ray. "It fucks some kids up for a long time. You fucked up about it?"

"Maybe," I said. I knelt. I kissed his forehead and then his lips. I was sober now. Clear. This felt as natural as anything. I liked my shaved skin. I liked having him take control over me. I liked him. But I didn't desire him. I thought I should desire him, but I didn't desire him.

"Are there others?" he said.

"I'm pretty sure. I was his favorite for a while, I think."

"You ever suicidal?" he said to me.

"I just live suicidally," I said.

"Well," he said softly, "lot's do."

"What do you do, Ray?" I said to him.

"I'm a doctor," he said. He held my wrists. He looked at me. There was a touch of gold in his brown eyes. He said, "Let's shut up and fuck."

I said, "All right."

Chapter Twenty-nine

All I had there were my girl clothes so I had to dress in them. I didn't wear the bra or the pantyhose. I walked barefoot in the dress, but I wore one of his long coats when we slipped out. He drove me to A&J's and we kissed good-bye in front of the house. I stood on my toes. He held my butt. "Good luck, kid," he said.

Inside everyone was still asleep. Flaming Joe was on the couch and woke up when I came in. "Whew," said Joe, pretending to wipe his forehead. "You really don't fuck around. No, I mean, you really *do* fuck around."

"Don't tell Rory," I said.

"I won't if you don't," said Joe.

Rory taught me how to drive his new Honda motorcycle. Then I got on back behind him and we drove to the University of Toledo where the basketball team held unofficial summer workouts. "I'm glad you're here. I want to beat these fuckers for a change," Rory said.

"Why?" I said.

"Old high school enemies. They think they're good. Division I. They care so much."

"So do you," I said.

"No!" said Rory.

We met a few of Rory's friends who played for Cornell and Columbia and scrimmaged against the Toledo varsity. I wore sweat pants and didn't shower so Rory wouldn't see that I'd shaved. We beat them and after the scrimmage one of the Toledo coaches came over and said to Rory, "Who's the ringer?"

Rory put his arm over my shoulder and laughed. "My friend," he said.

"Kind of a garbage man," the coach said to me.

"It doesn't matter how it goes in," I said.

"We don't see much of that on this level," he said.

"Fuck you," said Rory Gore. He shook my shoulder. "My friend, I love you," he said.

That night we picked up Flaming Joe and went to a striptease joint downtown.

"Is that all there is to do in this town?" I said.

"You should see Topeka," said Flaming Joe. "In Topeka they do it at lunch."

When I hitched back to Stuben I had so much to think about I couldn't think. I took a ride from a guy in a Corvair on his way to Youngstown. He looked like a hick—plaid, short-sleeve shirt, dark, greasy, receding hair combed straight back—but a couple miles down the road he asked me if I wanted a blow job.

"Ten bucks," I said to him.

When he pulled onto a side road, I said, "No, stay on the highway. Just pull off."

He blew me behind some shrubs and drove me all the way to Stuben.

Callahan was there when I got back and, of course, I went to him. He poured himself a scotch and sat down in his conversation chair. I got a bourbon and sat across from him. The first thing he did was show me a letter he just got from Kenny Bruce. Kenny was in Idaho. He'd dropped out of college, already married, with a kid, and divorced. He was penniless and homeless now, he said. "Help me, Mr. Callahan," he said. "Help me."

"What does he want?" Callahan said to me.

"Help," I said.

"With what? I sent him money. He sent it back."

"Survival," I said.

"Look how limited Wooj is," said Callahan. "Why do some people have it and some don't. It's a mystery to me."

"He wants you to tell him he's okay," I said. "That it's all okay."

"Of course it's okay!" said Callahan. "What's not okay? Only his refusal to take the world head on."

"It seems like it's taken him head on," I said.

"He never had it. He never had it in him," Callahan said. "He's a quitter."

I watched him. I thought about Luciani.

Dan took a breath. "What are you doing for money this summer, Mr. Rosenthal?" he said.

"I have a little left over from the scholarship benefits," I said.

"Did you have fun with your new guru up in Toledo?"

"Yes," I said. "We saw a striptease show."

"Not like the one in Nassau, I'm sure," said Dan. "You should have joined Wooj and me. We looked at a condominium."

"I had a pretty good time with Gil," I said.

"Well, that scholarship money won't last long," he said. "And you need another car."

"I'm thinking of buying a ten-speed bicycle."

"I can picture you in the winter," said Callahan. "Listen. I have a job lined up for you at the Census Bureau. A few hours a night. You can make a thousand dollars. And I lined up a car. Tom Ketching down at Ketching Motors has a used MG there. You remember him, he's a Holy Name kid. He'll sell it to you for what it costs him to turn it over. We can finance it like before."

I sipped my drink. "Thank you," I said. "I'll take the job, but let me finance the car on my own."

"Fine. Suit yourself," Callahan said. "It's good to have you around again. Drop by the gym."

"I will," I said.

He wasn't vice-president of St. Mary's anymore. He was dean again, but now the only dean. He talked about Holy Name. Another city football championship. A state title in boys' basketball. But the population base had gone down in the center city. There'd be no Gold Team on the J.V. level next year. "I told Sam," he said. "He didn't seem to mind." He talked about my family some, how they were stubborn and had an inordinate sense of justice. "It must be crowded in that room with your brothers," he said.

"Not as crowded as it was with Gil in there," I said.

"How about a dorm room up at St. Mary's?" said Dan. "It's summer. The place is empty."

We got in his car, but first we drove to the river front, along the beach where I used to sneak off with Linda Thomas. It was dusk and it reminded me of the time I swam in front of him in Columbus. How he held me afterward. We crossed the bridge and stared across the river at the city. "It's a beautiful little town," Dan said.

"See those factories there. I'm going to transform that area into an historical museum, and a new public library."

"You love this place," I said.

"Love?" said Dan Callahan. "It's a little city, Mr. Rosenthal. If I left, they'd forget about me in six months. At Holy Name and St. Mary's, too."

"Then why do it?"

"Altruism, Mr. Rosenthal," he said. "Altruism. Don't let anyone ever tell you it doesn't exist."

I think he believed it. We drove to the campus. We walked through the halls of the new dorm. He was so proud of it. When we got to the dorm room, it reminded me of my rooms at Ohio State. No refrigerator, no hot plate, no radio, no lamps, no phone, a bathroom down the hall. "Consider it a refuge," said Dan Callahan. "If you need food or a drink, drop by my place." His place, for all I needed.

When we got back to his house I made another drink. I sat across from him again. "I took a blow job hitch-hiking," I said to him.

"No," said Dan. "No. Where?"

"On the side of the road. I charged ten bucks."

"How could you do that?"

"The blow job?" I said, baiting him.

"The money," he said. "Mr. Rosenthal, you prostituted yourself."

"Sex for gifts," I said to him.

"I'm disappointed in you, Mr. Rosenthal. I've done better by you than to have you whore yourself on the side of the road."

I was a pretty hairless kid, but in bed that night Callahan didn't even seem to notice the stubble on my legs. That night, humping him, I thought about Toledo, and Ray. With Ray, I hadn't imagined myself as a girl. "You fucked up about it?" Ray had asked me. "You fucked up about it?" Christ, was I fucked up.

Chapter Thirty

⎯⎯⎯∞⎯⎯⎯

The census job was hell. We were supposed to conduct phone in-
terviews with high school kids about their plans for the future;
whether or not they planned to stay in Stuben and why. They were
never home, so I'd make arrangements with their parents to meet
them at their house, but when I'd get there they'd already have
left. I was working eight hours a day, not four, and in three weeks
I was behind on my quota.

That summer I tried to stay in shape. I worked out at St. Mary's
new auditorium with their varsity at the unofficial practices. All
those kids had summer jobs in Stuben. Callahan had hired my old
coach, Larry LaRuche. My all-around game was maturing and I
spent time working on my passing game, particularly the bounce
pass. On defense I practiced triangulating myself between my man
and the ball handler in order to anticipate passes for steals.

LaRuche took me aside after one scrimmage. "I've never seen
anyone as disciplined as you about their game," he said to me.

"I have to be," I said. "I don't have the talent."

"You really think that?"

"Ask Callahan."

"Aah, Callahan, our benefactor." He chuckled. "You thinking
of coming here, Chuck?" he said to me.

"I don't know," I said to him. "All your guys have to play to
keep their scholarships."

He scratched his chin. "Those academic scholarships can be
pretty fragile things, too," he said.

I said, "Maybe, but you've got to believe in something."

He put his arm over my shoulder and chuckled. "Well,
Rosenthal, you've always marched to your own drum," he said.

"Do you think?" I said.

He laughed more. He laughed pretty hard.

I didn't buy the MG. I picked up a used motorcycle, a 400cc Suzuki, and drove that thing all over the place. Staying in the dorm kept me in touch with the St. Mary's summer school party life and more often than not, if I didn't end up on somebody's floor or in their bed, I crashed in the dorm. Or I slept with Callahan. He had a new friend now, a high school kid who'd played on his third state title team and now played forward for Stuben Tech, probably the best team in the city that year. He was well built and had thick, blond hair that swooped down over his forehead. He wasn't the brightest guy in the world, but Callahan said he was a working class kid, like me. His father was a cop. That's the kind of kid he liked to help. His name was Carson McDonnell. I saw him when I showed up at night, sitting in the chair across from Callahan, the place where I always sat; I guess where everybody did.

"You young men know each other, don't you?" Callahan said the first night I ran into them. "Mr. McDonnell. Mr. Rosenthal."

Carson got up and we shook hands.

"I expect you to be his role model, Mr. Rosenthal," Callahan said.

Carson grinned at me. He tilted his head and knit his brow ever so slightly. It wasn't a look of admiration, but of cynicism.

One night I arrived at Callahan's early, a little after eleven. As usual, I let myself in by the back door and made myself a drink. I heard rummaging upstairs and sat there drinking for over and hour before Callahan and Carson emerged from the walled stairway. Carson offered me his sly nod and Callahan said, "Ah, Mr. Rosenthal. Let me take Carson home and I'll be right with you."

I had another drink, then another, before Dan came in the door. "It's getting pretty late," he said to me, "we better get right upstairs."

When I didn't move he said, "What, Mr. Rosenthal?"

"Do you love me, Dan?" I said to him.

He sputtered. Hesitated. "Get upstairs," he said.

I said it again. "Do you love me?"

He chuckled and shook his head. He put his hands on his hips. "Mr. Rosenthal, what are you talking about?"

"Love," I said. "Isn't that why we do what we do?"

"We don't do anything, Mr. Rosenthal."

"Upstairs," I said. "The sex."

"Are you crazy?" Callahan said.

"I don't have anything against homosexuality," I said to him. "For all I know I am a homosexual." I turned my back on him and went to the kitchen. I dumped my ice, got more from the freezer, poured out another glass of Jack Daniels.

"You are not a homosexual," said Dan Callahan. "You know nothing about homosexuality."

"I think I do," I said.

"A blow job on the side of the road?"

"What you and I have done a thousand times."

"That is therapy!" screamed Callahan. "Do you think I enjoy that? I do it for you."

"For me."

"You think I don't have better things to do than poke and prod your body to make you a basketball player?"

"Altruism," I said.

"Yes!"

"I think you're manipulative, Dan, and I think you lie to yourself."

"Think twice, Chuck Rosenthal," Dan Callahan said. "I don't make anyone do anything. But you still need me. You don't know how much. But if you want to walk away, I won't hold you. You're free. Suit yourself."

"I should have learned to play the piano," I said.

"What are you talking about?"

"I should have learned the piano!" I screamed at him. "Instead of basketball. Basketball made me a whore!"

"You little bastard," said Callahan. "You ungrateful bastard."

"I am not ungrateful," I said softly. "I'm sorry."

He didn't say anything and we stood there quietly. "All right," he finally said. "Forget about it. Now get upstairs."

"Do you love me?" I said.

"What are you talking about!" screamed Callahan.

I took a deep drink. "I feel you get hard, Dan," I said. "I feel you come."

"Get out of here!" Callahan yelled. He raised his fist at me and I blocked it. He tried to hit me again, but I was bigger than him, stronger and faster. I blocked his flailing blow again, then turned and left. I got on the bike and drove to the Census Office where I averaged out the first third of my work and filled in the other two-thirds of the forms myself on par with the other answers. Then I drove to my dorm room, grabbed all the acid I had and downed it in a gulp. Maybe it was enough to kill me or drive me mad, I didn't know. I got on the bike again and hit the freeway. I was still pretty drunk but I started getting off in an hour and in another hour the acid peaked as I drove through downtown Cincinnati, the lights of the skyscrapers shining like Oz. Out in the dark between Cincinnati and Indianapolis the road fell away like a black ribbon, the drone of the bike arose like the song of the spheres, the stripes and reflectors flew beneath my headlight, lifted me up, flying, flying amid starlight, the road a path in stars.

Chapter Thirty-one

———⟨∞⟩———

"Hello," said Sonya Pulski over the phone.

"I'm here," I said.

"Here?"

"In East St. Louis."

"You are not here," Sony Pulski said. "You are *there*."

"Come see. I'm at this great breakfast joint on Washington and 3rd," I said.

"You're on Washington and 3rd and you're still alive?"

"The place is full of living people," I said. "Where do you live? I'll come get you."

She gave me directions and I drove to her suburb outside St. Louis where she was waiting for me on her gigantic lawn.

"You look horrible," she said.

"I feel horrible," I said.

I still had a pretty good buzz, but I was getting hungry. We drove back to East St. Louis and ate pancakes, sausages, grits and fried greens.

"I love black people," said Sonya Pulski. "Why haven't I ever realized that?"

"Anyone in particular?" I said.

"Real people, like this," she said.

"I guess you can be nobody to everybody," I said.

"I don't know what that means, but I like it," said Sonya.

"You're being facetious."

"Is that a word I should know?"

"Is it?"

"Do I say all my smart things when you're not around?"

"Should I answer that?" I said.

"Can we go fuck somewhere?"

"Your house."

"My parents will hate you, even if you shower. And we have a black maid."

"I need to sleep," I said.

She called home and when her mother was gone we drove to the suburbs. I showered, then slept in a hammock in the backyard. Her father, Lawrence, wore a toupee. Her mother, Pat, was a Presbyterian like Cameron Marney. They had a living room that no one was allowed to go in. The plastic was still on the lamp shades. Lawrence gave me a Coors that he'd had imported from Colorado and took me outside to watch him barbecue huge steaks. The smoke rose between us and burned my eyes.

"You're not some kind of vegetarian," he said

"No kind," I said. "Would it change anything about dinner?"

"No. You got a job?"

"I play basketball."

"That's not a job."

"It's a job," I said.

"Do you support the war?"

"I hate the war."

"God?"

"Atheist."

"Do you like the beer?"

"Thank you, but no, I can barely taste the beer."

"You're an asshole," he said.

"No," I said, "you're an asshole."

He flipped the steak. "You can sleep in the basement, but I want you gone in the morning," he said.

"Thank you," I said.

But later, after he went to bed, I sneaked upstairs and fucked his daughter, and she me, in the room across from his.

"How'd you like my dad?" Sonya Pulski asked. She liked to fuck sitting up on the floor.

"He's an asshole," I said.

"That's my dad," said Sonya Pulski.

"I didn't mention I was Jewish."

"Or black, thank fucking God," Sonya said.

That fall, back in Manfred, Sonya Pulski moved into my place. She kept her dorm room because that's what Lawrence and Pat were paying for. I lived off campus in an alley about six blocks from the school. I didn't move into the athletic dorm. Rory was gone now, and Flaming Joe, too, so I was tripping less often. I got stoned and drunk with Marvin Wilson and the other blacks.

"Gore is gone so you black now," Marvin said.

"We can't just hang out?"

"You living with a white chick. What happened with the sister?"

"That ended a long time ago. I've dated some other black chicks."

"I liked you better when you were just white."

"I am white."

"Fucking straight you're white," said Marvin. "Whitey," Marvin said.

Four of the black players from last year left for other programs, but Marvin and three others stayed, and there were three black freshman. That fall, for the first time ever, Manfred would likely start more blacks than whites. Whatever you wanted to say about Crowder, his hard realism made him recruit blacks.

But the unofficial practices were hell. Crowder let it be known that all the starting jobs were wide open. He ran rebounding and ball possession drills where he called no fouls. We just had to fight it out. Things got rough and bloody and I dreaded showing up. But I was trying to hold myself together. I was good at basketball. I wasn't good at anything else. I tried to separate it from Callahan, the way I tried to keep my fantasy life—for which I'd learned the word in my psychology class, transsexual—at a distance from real sex. There were no gay clubs in the town of Manfred. Not in rural Ohio. Not that I'd go. I didn't know what sex I was, what I wanted to be or who or what I desired, but I knew I could play basketball. In the end, Crowder would play me because I was the best player he had.

Crowder hadn't said anything about where I lived, but he set the haircut deadline for November 1, the first official practice. The campus was still torn, and everywhere I went both jocks and freaks asked me if I was going to cut my hair, if I was going to play. Like Rory, I told them it wasn't about hair. If I decided to play, I'd cut it. But now, with Rory gone, between me and Crowder it really did come down to hair.

Halloween night, Sonya and I got pretty loaded and some time near dawn I went into the bathroom, shaved, then came out and handed her a pair of scissors. "Go to it, baby," I said and she gave me the worst haircut in the history of the world. It met regulations, falling above my ears, but the top was twenty different lengths. Sonya ran out at daylight and came back with five different hair dyes. She dyed it red, yellow, black, white, brown.

"It's within regulations," I said.

"You look like the future," said Sonya.

That night at practice I cut a pretty wide swathe. Only Marvin came up to me as I shot around at a side basket.

"I got to hand it to you," he said. "You don't give a shit how you look."

"On the contrary," I said. "I do."

Crowder came onto the floor and blew his whistle. He stood in front of us, but when his eyes rested on me everybody snickered.

"Rosenthal," he said. "In my office."

We didn't even sit down. He stood in front of me, not quite my height.

"What do you think you're doing?" Crowder said.

"It's within regulations. Sir," I said.

"Do I look like a fool, Rosenthal?"

"No, Coach," I said. "I do."

He heaved in front of me. He turned sideways and looked at me with one eye. "I thought we'd talked in the spring," he said.

"Yes," I said. "We did."

"Get out of here," he said. "Come back tomorrow with a decent haircut."

The options were dropping like flies. Last spring, in philosophy, I'd read Sartre's "Existentialism Is a Humanism." Sartre said that when people wanted advice, they went to get it from people who would tell them what they'd already decided. It was a warm November 1st night and I'd vowed I'd ride my motorcycle till the snow fell. Though it had been over two months, I bundled up and drove to Stuben to see Callahan.

Chapter Thirty-two

⎯⎯⎯∞∞∞⎯⎯⎯

"Mr. Rosenthal," Callahan said when he came to the door, "what the hell have you done to your hair?"

"Haircut," I said.

"And Crowder didn't accept it," Callahan laughed. "Chuck Rosenthal, you are a lightning rod for trouble." He chuckled and turned. "Come in. Have a drink. It's great to see you."

"No drink," I said. "I need to hear why I should play."

"Play?" said Callahan. "Don't be absurd. You've worked seven years for this moment. Seven years, day and night."

Yes, I thought, day and night. "I don't want to fight with Crowder all season." I followed Dan into his living room and we sat.

"What will you do if you don't play?" he asked.

"Become a scholar," I said.

"Scholars, Mr. Rosenthal, have tremendous discipline."

"I have discipline."

He offered a doubtful rise of one eybrow. "And first rate minds. You've yet to demonstrate that. The rigor and politics of the academy would drive you up a wall. You'd never last."

"What will I do after two more years of basketball?" I said. "I can't play pro."

"Not in the U.S. But you could play in Europe. It would be educational and you'd buy yourself time to mature."

I sat forward with my elbows on my knees. "I don't enjoy it anymore," I said.

"That's just Rory Gore talking," Dan said. "And where is he? Working for the railroad. Waiting to be drafted. The closer you get to the season, Crowder will go to you more and more. The first time you send the ball through the hoop and the crowd roars, you'll feel it again. Before that, you'll feel it. It will come back."

"I'm tired," I said.

"You are not tired, Mr. Rosenthal. You are too young to be tired. You've got that girl now. You're feeling secure. But if you quit basketball and she leaves you, you'll have nothing. You'll be nothing. You'll have nothing to fall back on. It happened before, but you had basketball. What happens when you wake up tomorrow or next week and find out you didn't want to quit? What will happen years from now when you want to relive what you gave up? You have this opportunity now and never again."

He went on like that for a while. I thought he'd argue for me to come to St. Mary's, but he didn't. He was thinking about me. About what was best for me. He knew me. He knew what I could do. What I wanted. "Everyone on campus will know your name. You'll leave Manfred as the greatest scorer in their history. And that will help you later when you go out in the world. You'll be recognized. Known. If you want to go to graduate school, there's your ticket to grad school. Use your head, Mr. Rosenthal. For once, use your head."

I sat back. "All right," I said. "That's what I came to hear."

"You made the right choice," Dan Callahan said to me. "You made the right choice. Now get upstairs and let's make sure that body of yours is ready to back it up."

I thought of saying no, but he'd helped me and I didn't want to fight. It was what I gave back to him for all he did for me. "I'll have that drink now," I said.

"Fine," he said. "Fine. How's your family?"

I got up and went into his kitchen. Before pouring myself a huge drink, I swilled from the bottle. I felt calmer, warmer, bolstered. "Pour me a scotch and water, will you?" Dan said, and I did. I brought it in. "I worry about your brother Joe," he said.

"His size?" I said. "Andy's almost as big and only in sixth grade."

"It's not just his size. Andy has an athlete's temperament," Callahan said. "Joe is weak. No matter how I push or prod him, he never steps up. He's such a pretty boy. Maybe he's too pretty."

"I'll talk to him," I said.

"I hope you do," Dan Callahan said.

That night, as I he held my mouth to his and I plunged between his thighs, I felt his penis rise under his jockeys and I imagined myself as Sonya. I thought of Ray and how easy it was with

Ray. What kind of life could I live with Sonya Pulski or anyone? What would Sonya think if she knew? What would anyone think?

In the morning I drove to Sam and Helen's. I knew they'd be grocery shopping, so it would give me a chance to talk to Joe alone. I went inside. It was quiet. I walked upstairs. The bedroom door was closed, so I tapped it lightly and walked in. Joe and Andy sat on the floor. They were passing a joint. They both held Budweisers. They looked up at me with their half-closed eyes and Andy offered me the joint.

"It's a little early," I said. "And you guys are pretty young."

"It's a little late for advice," said Andy.

"Want a beer?" said Joe.

"Don't you guys have basketball practice soon?"

"This is how we get through it," Andy said.

"Basketball practice?"

"What team did you play on?" said Andy.

"To be able to face him," said Joe.

"Callahan?" I said.

It got quiet. Andy hit on the joint and passed it to Joe. Joe smoked. Exhaled. "It's walking in there," Joe finally said. "Walking in there with him. No one ever says anything, but everybody knows."

"Knows what?"

"The sex!" screamed Joe. "The fucking sex!" He began to weep.

"You shouldn't have got him started," Andy said to me.

"The fucking sperm and Vaseline," wept Joe. "You can't wash it off you. You can never get it off!"

I looked at Andy who said, "Hey, I don't get molested. He just grabs my balls and spanks me."

"Oh Jesus," I said. "Oh Christ."

"You thought it was just you?" Andy said.

I took the beer and sat there with them. I smoked with them. Joe wept quietly and we didn't say anything for a long time.

"You don't have to go back," I said to them.

"We're in too deep," said Joe.

"I'll go to Callahan now and tell him you're not coming back," I said. "I'll quit, too."

"You don't have to quit for us," Andy said. He hit on the joint, exhaled. "I'm going to be a star. That's my road. I'm not afraid of Callahan. There's no other way."

"You don't want to be a fucking sports star, Andy," I said.

"I do," Andy said. "You can't fucking tell me."

"Joe?" I said.

"Nobody's ever quit on him," Joe whispered. "The parents, the kids, they'll take me apart."

I finished the beer and put it in front of me. I got up. "I'm quitting, Joe," I said.

"You can't," said Joe. "Look at who you are. It's everything."

"I'm quitting," I said to him. "What should I tell him about you?"

He thought for a minute. He pulled on the beer. "Tell him I never want to see him again," Joe said. "I'm done."

I caught Callahan in his driveway, preparing to leave for practice.

"Mr. Rosenthal," he said, "is something wrong?"

I did not know what to say. I didn't know how to broach the irony of what would be perceived as my betrayal, and Joe's. I'd raced there on the bike, enraged, and now I saw, like Joe, how deep it was, as deep as my past and my future, as deep as all I had been and all I could be.

"Mr. Rosenthal?" he said.

"I'm quitting, Dan."

"I thought we settled that last night."

"We did," I said to him. "Joe's quitting, too."

"Are you boys crazy?" he said. "Tell Joe to get his ass to practice. And you get back to Manfred."

"We're done with all of it, Dan," I said. "At least Joe and I are."

He paused for a moment. He tilted his head slightly. "You can't hurt me, Mr. Rosenthal," he said. "You can't touch me."

"I don't want to touch you," I said to him. "Or have you touch me. Or Joe. Ever again. We're done." I didn't want to go further with it. We'd been through it before. He could admit none of it. And it was clear to me now that there was no quitting one without quitting both.

"You'll regret this." Callahan raised his finger. "You'll come crawling back in a day. You'll end up at St. Mary's or you'll be fighting in that war you despise so much."

"I quit," I said, and turned away. I got on the bike and drove home.

Sam and Helen seemed almost relieved.

"It's your choice," said Sam. "It's your life. Study."

"What about Andy?" said Helen.

"He's staying with it for now," I said.

"Andy's a tough kid. He'll be fine," said Sam.

I saw, in their faces—even if they didn't know about Dan Callahan and what he did with their kids, and who could ever tell them?—an understanding that I couldn't have had until just then, that for everything they now wouldn't get, there was something else they wouldn't owe.

Compared to all that, Crowder, if enraged, was easy.

"Your hair, Rosenthal," he said when I walked into his office.

"It's not about hair, Coach," I said.

"I told you not to come back without a haircut."

"I'm not coming back," I said. "I just came to tell you."

"What the hell are you talking about?"

"Coach, it's about everything and it just ended here, that's all," I said.

"Everything what? It's simple. Play basketball."

"I can't do it anymore, Coach," I said to him. "It's not just politics or hair or whether or not you and I can get along. It's way beyond that."

"Listen, Rosenthal. Forget about the hair. We can talk about it later."

"It's not about hair, Coach," I said. "I have to quit everything I was up till now and find out who I am."

"You can't do that and play basketball?"

"No," I said, "I can't."

That night I didn't drink. I went to bed and slept hard and deep until almost Sunday dusk. I looked out the window into the gray light turning dark and couldn't realize how I would one day envision the hell behind and the hell ahead. I was relieved and depressed and scared, and already regretted quitting and walking away from the only thing I'd ever been.

Sonya came home and rubbed my neck. "Looks like somebody quit something," she said.

"Yes," I said, not looking up.

"You are major quixotic," she said.

In the morning we took the bike up to school and checked our mail before heading to class. There was a letter for me from the academic vice-president. He had been informed, and he'd confirmed, that I was in violation of my scholarship code by owning a motor vehicle. I'd lost my scholarship.

"You don't get a trial?" Sonya said.

"Informed and confirmed."

"Who knew?" Sonya said. "Crowder?"

"I don't know," I said. "Maybe Crowder. Maybe somebody else." I thought of Callahan. I looked at the letter again. "Maybe everybody."

"I didn't know those guys worked weekends," she said.

"It's fast," I said.

"What are you going to do?" Sonya said to me. "You'll be drafted. You'll have to play someplace else."

"No," I said. "I'm not playing anywhere else."

She took my hand. "I have to go. I'm late. You going to be all right?"

"Yes," I said.

"All right." She kissed me and went off.

I looked at the letter again. I wasn't going back to basketball. I wasn't going back to Callahan. I didn't know what I was going to do, but I'd do something. As Rory Gore might say, some things end, others begin.

Epilogue

One of the differences between stories and life is that stories end and life goes on, even after death. Even after you die people have to bury you and fold up your stuff and look at your pictures and tell stories about you or ignore you or forget you, all things I tried to do with that boy, Chuck Rosenthal, who at nineteen stood at the edge of admitting what had been done to him, yet managed to deny the horror.

Because you don't start having sex with someone at thirteen and just stop at nineteen. You don't just walk away. You carry it inside and live with it, hide it, go back to it, ignore it, fail to ignore it; you live with shame; you try to normalize what happened. From age nineteen till forty-five, I told myself that it was homosexual sex and there was nothing wrong with it. That I had consented. That sex was the price of Callahan's friendship and patronage. That his unresolved sexuality was his business. My unresolved sexuality was my business and my responsibility. For thirty years I stood where Chuck Rosenthal stands at the end of this story, never really admitting what had been done to me, and denying the horror, even into the early drafts of this memoir, which initially began to exonerate Callahan, and was at first entitled *Consenting Child*. I've got hundreds pages laying around somewhere, pages that tried to talk about those thirty years, so you can imagine how inadequate I feel trying to explain myself here.

I finished college by securing loans. I turned down several scholarship offers to play basketball, including one from Larry LaRuche. By my senior year I'd learned the term *transsexual* and in my twenties I was convinced that I was transsexual and bisexual, a conviction that I hid from Sonya, to whom I was briefly married. That's where I placed my shame and guilt. I was confused and ashamed of my transsexual fantasies and ashamed, too, for hiding them. As my marriage fell apart, I experimented with homosexuality and heterosexuality, as often as not with equal inconsistency and frustration. I drank heavily every day. I took almost every drug you can name. I began to take risks with my life.

After getting an M.A. in philosophy, I returned to Stuben. Callahan, still Dean of St. Mary's College, had hired me to teach. I fell in with him again. I was a consenting adult then. My homosexuality was my own business, even if his was his own secret, even to himself. He was my boss, my patron, my friend. I tried to shrug off the sex. If I was unsteady about my lack of attraction for men, I became equally unsteady about my lack of enthusiasm for most women (I didn't know that this asexual response was one of many symptoms of sexual abuse in men). But Callahan's sexual duplicity and manipulative domination became intolerable again. After my mother died of cancer, I finally left Stuben for good.

For three years in Northern California I pushed the limits of drug abuse and sexual conduct. On a number of occasions, dangerously fucked up, I took tremendous risks, diving from bridges and cliffs, climbing girders at construction sites, taking acid on my motorcycle. I told myself that I was just a wild guy who couldn't face turning thirty. I didn't think that these were symptoms of sexual abuse, that sometimes you're willing to kill yourself in order to kill a part of yourself you can't live with. In those years I began to rebuild some sexual confidence and became somewhat notorious, though one night after a party my roommate, a gay man, said to me, "You spent the night dick teasing my friends." When I didn't respond he said, "Chuck, quit trying to be gay. You're heterosexual. It's all right to be straight." And he was right.

A year later I was in grad school in Utah where I met Gail, who I've been with for twenty years. In the first ten of those years, though I never had sex with Callahan again, I remained his friend. Gail and I got our Ph.D.'s from Utah and took jobs teaching in Los Angeles. Callahan had become president of St. Mary's and he often brought me in to teach or give readings. I'm embarrassed to admit that Gail and I were married one summer in the vestibule of St. Mary's College chapel. Sometimes, when visiting Callahan while I was home, a young man would show up late at night and I would leave and he would stay. Or in the afternoon, a shy, freshly scrubbed young boy would stalk Callahan's living room, eyes cast downward. I recognized that shame.

Except for my parents, who I never told (I have only recently told my siblings besides Andrew and Joe), I was honest with everyone else about my sexual past, including Gail. I'd had sex with my basketball coach and mentor for ten years. I was bisexual another ten. That was that. Gail resented Callahan. She tried to give me a lot of space, but after our wedding she avoided him when at all possible. Then, well into my forties, a number of events changed everything. My brother, Joe, who'd come out to Los Angeles for his job, had a nervous breakdown and lived with us, almost helpless, for a year and a half. My daughter was growing toward puberty and I began to ask myself if I'd permit her to have sex, like I did, with an adult. My closest friend at the time was a lawyer. When I told him about my having sex with Callahan he said, "You were sexually abused." No one had ever said that to me. "I consented," I said to him. He said, "You were a child. You couldn't consent. It was statutory rape."

Now, in my mid-forties, I began to reconsider my sexual childhood. Soon after, while I was conceiving *Never Let Me Go*, Joe broke down in our living room, sobbing. He talked about Callahan's physical abuse and sadism, the hand jobs, the Vaseline, the humping face to face. Suddenly I saw Joe as a forty-year-old man who had no job, no home, no lover, a man broken by something in his past, and I felt the horror for him that I never felt for myself. The next day, when Gail turned to me and said, "Joe was sexually abused. He was raped and so were you," the tenor of my memoir changed. I spent two years writing my way toward trying to understand what had happened to me—hundreds and hundreds of pages— and when I was done I spent six months in therapy.

I wish I had a checklist for avoiding sexual abuse, or a manual for surviving it. But if you are alive, then you have survived. I say this because many victims commit suicide. If you aren't a drug addict, an alcoholic, if you aren't hysterical or insane, then you're better off than many. You might yet be sexually confused, several times divorced, alone, helpless and broken. At worst, you might now be a sexual molester yourself.

I don't know how to teach someone to reach into his heart. I do know that it's okay to have been sexually molested as a child. It wasn't your fault, though the consequences have likely been devastating. But if you are not to blame for what you have become, you are yet responsible for what you will become. Face it. Forgive yourself. Get help.

I hesitate to point to myself as a model of survival, because I can't tell you how or why I survived, nor do I believe that I am the one to assess the quality of my own life. Mostly I was lucky; lucky not to have died from drugs, alcohol, AIDS, or risks; lucky that I found a companion and lover; lucky to have a loving family. I am lucky to have a passion for writing that has kept me busy almost every day for the last twenty-five years. I found fulfilling work: teaching. I exercise daily, running in the mountains and riding my horse. I love animals. These things keep me alive.

When I was twenty-one I discovered Buddhism. I seldom talk about it with anyone, particularly Buddhists, but I have kept a personal practice for thirty years. It has given me detachment from events, sympathy for life, perspective on my past. So if I were to offer any advice at all it would be to find people to love, animals to love, things you love to do, help others, live life religiously. Face your past. Forgive yourself. Get counseling.

No one gets through life undamaged or unscarred, but sometimes I go looking for the unmolested boy of twelve inside me who was inquisitive, athletic, religious, intelligent, and already a good writer. Those things, I think, have not changed. I don't know if Callahan made me a basketball player. But contrary to everything he always told me, I believe that I already possessed the discipline to be successful athletically, intellectually, and creatively. His underestimation of me, including his insistence on my "B+ mind," was a means of keeping me dependent on him, because it was essential that I believed, even into adulthood, that I could not succeed without him in order to keep me close and keep me quiet.

There are emotional scars that I feel are integrally related to my sexual molestation. For years I lacked confidence in every aspect of my life, intellectually, sexually, athletically. Subsequently, to this day I am often incapable of taking credit for my accomplishments, including, Gail would argue, surviving my molestation. The years of living a hidden, unspeakable life, of day-in, day-out psycho-sexual dependence produced deep insecurities and made me very susceptible to over-dependency in sexual relationships. The grave violation of my naïve trust made me misanthropic. I do not trust people. I do not know if I was a stoic child, but I became a stoic adult, so much so that to this day I often find it impossible to know what I feel about something, a result, I'm certain, of years of emotional repression. I later learned that many molested children, unable to face the horror of the act, create an alternative personality to get through it, thus my transsexual fantasies which are a permanent part of my psyche. I have learned since, through study and through counseling, that transsexuality is not transvestitism. Neither necessarily implies the other, nor do your fantasies necessarily imply that you hope or wish for your fantasies to be real. I find nothing wrong with homosexuality, in fact I am pleased to have had homosexual experiences, but trying to find my inherent heterosexuality beneath the maelstrom, well, it was long, hard, confusing, and painful. While a teenager, I often thought that Callahan was the victim of my perversity, because I knowingly used him for homosexual sex while he didn't even know he was having it.

I can only speak for myself and never witnessed Callahan having sex with any other boys. But in recent months I have heard about other men from my home town, and spoken to a few. There are probably very many. And I think they are silenced to this day by shame, manipulation, threats, fear, favors, dependence, denial, and repression. I never considered prosecuting or suing Callahan because it has only been in the last five years that I thought anything really wrong had happened. Besides, until very recently, I didn't know I could sue and since, the Supreme Court has ruled against such suits. Even before that, when I spoke to a lawyer, I was told that my accomplishments, my intelligence, and my open-mindedness mitigated my suffering and symptoms, and the fact that I didn't repress the molestation, but was always aware that the sex occurred, made me susceptible to the statute of limitations.

Sexual molestation of children, particularly of boys by men, is a silenced plague in our culture, because men can't be victims; they can't admit it has happened to them and we can't admit it has happened to our men.

If you have children, including teenagers, under the supervision of adults, whether they are coaches, scout leaders, teachers, or clerics, then learn to supervise the supervisors. Your kids should not be spending long periods of time alone with an adult, certainly not at night. Individual adults should not be spending unsupervised time with a child or even groups of children or teenagers. There should always be at least two adults involved. Are single, childless adults more suspicious? Unfortunately, yes.

Err on the side of caution. Once molestation begins there is nowhere for a child or teenager to turn, because they are powerless; they are ashamed and scared and have everything to lose. And people don't want to know. Despite all the recent press about the sexual abuse of boys by priests, few secular cases of man-boy sexual abuse have been successfully prosecuted. Listen to me. I speak from experience. Even now, you doubt me.